THE WHOLESALING
BLUEPRINT

Real Estate Investing with
No Money Out of Your Pocket

LUKE WEBER

This book is dedicated to my team and to you.
We all win together!

CONTENTS

Introduction

Action Brings Success.

As I sit in my office making the final revisions to this book, I am negotiating a wholesale deal that will put $21,000 in my pocket. A seller contacted me wanting $140,000 for their home, we signed a contract at $115,000 and I have a buyer willing to pay $136,000 for the property. Why did that seller contact me? How did I know how much to offer? Where did I find a "real" buyer? How does that $21,000 get into my pocket? All of these questions and more will be answered within these pages so that you can do this too. Are you ready to change your life? Are you ready to take action? Then keep reading!

Two years ago, I wrote my book *The Flipping Blueprint* and it quickly became the number-one book in the country on how to flip houses. I wrote *The Flipping Blueprint* because I received hundreds of questions from new and experienced investors from all over the country on how I did what I do and how could they do it too. By nature, I am a helper and I want to answer people's questions, but it became difficult to answer everyone's questions because there just wasn't enough time! Additionally, I found I was answering the same questions over and over from different people, and it took a ton of time away from my business and, most importantly, my family. I would be out with my family and those unanswered questions lingered in my mind as something I still needed to finish. I like to help people, but I also like to work efficiently. That's when I decided to write my first book.

Just like in my real estate investing business, I wanted to automate as much as possible so I had more time to spend with my family and do the things that I love, but still be able to help people. I started writing, and writing, and writing. I put as much detail, tips, and tricks as I could into the pages, yet still have it make sense both for someone first starting in real estate investing and the seasoned professionals out there too. I covered everything from finding deals to designing houses to estimating rehabs to reselling your properties for maximum profit, and now there are investors in markets all over the country making massive profits because of these tips and tricks. But, flipping houses is not for everyone. Just because flipping is a huge source of income for me, doesn't mean that is what you want to do, and that is probably why you are reading this book. Additionally, flipping houses is not my only business or source of income. Just like before, I still receive a lot of questions about wholesaling real estate: how people can get started, where to find properties, and how to sell them. If something works, repeat it. My first book worked and recovered my time, and it helped (and is helping) a lot of people, so why wouldn't I write a book on another subject and help even more people achieve their dreams of financial freedom?

In this book, I am going to focus on wholesaling real estate, the business of selling your interest in a contract to a third party for profit (don't worry about the terminology, we'll go into more detail in the next chapter!). Wholesaling is the best way to get quick and easy money from real estate with no money out of your own pocket, if you believe all of the glamour stories on social media and from self-proclaimed experts. Now, let's be clear from the very start, you can do this business with no money out of your own pocket, but having some money for marketing and building systems will help you along. What the sub header of this book (*Real Estate Investing with No Money out of your Pocket*) really means is that you will be involved in real estate transactions without bringing the money to buy the property. It will still take money out of your pocket to grow this business but, ideally, that can all be done from the proceeds from those first deals that you hustle and grind to get. I'll explain how you can do that within these pages. I have done hundreds of wholesale deals all across the country, both as a buyer and as a seller, and have experienced the easy, the hard, and the crazy deals. Now I want to share my experiences with you and show you how to actually get into this business with little to no money and start making profits now!

Here's a little more about me for those who haven't read *The Flipping Blueprint*. I am a former real estate appraiser. I bought my first house in 2003 and flipped it for a profit of more than $80,000, and I was hooked! I have bought and sold rental portfolios, flipped hundreds of houses all over the country, and I buy anything real estate related that I can make money on. From land to condos to manufactured homes to apartment buildings and everything in between (I've even flipped a church!), if I can make money on it, I buy it!

I travel the world with my wonderful wife and amazing son. When I am not doing that, I have a real estate-investing firm (learn those words!), a real estate brokerage, and a construction company that I grow along with a few other businesses. I play soccer and cook, I go to my son's hockey games, and I have coffee dates with my wife. Basically, I get to do what I want, when I want. Now, this didn't happen overnight, and it won't last forever if I walk away from it. Don't be fooled, your real estate business will take work and continued action. If you aren't feeding and growing your business, who will?

So why did I write another book? Why am I sharing even more secrets? *Why not?* I live a life of abundance. I know there are enough deals out there for everyone and we can all win together. Who knows? Maybe someday, you and I will do a deal together? I still buy properties from wholesalers and I still train new wholesalers how to find me more deals. That's right, I train my competition because I don't believe they are competition. They are compatriots, co-workers, and part of my team! They are strategic partners who will help me further grow my real estate-investing firm. Why wouldn't I want them to have more skills in finding properties? Why wouldn't I want to buy a property from you? The more I help you, the more chance you can help me. It's really that simple. And besides, just like when I wrote my book, *The Flipping Blueprint*, I get a lot of questions about wholesaling. Remember, if something works, repeat it!

CHAPTER 1

Wholesaling, So What Is It Really?

Wholesaling is the art of selling your interest in a contract to a third party for profit. Let's break that down a little bit more, but don't forget, this truly is an art form. You can be really good at it and sell your art next to a Picasso or a Van Gogh for the big bucks, or you can just be doing funny drawings of tourists for tips on a boardwalk somewhere. Which do you want to be?

Let's do a quick breakdown of the basic parts of a wholesale deal. There are four main components to a wholesale transaction:

1. The Property

2. The Contract

3. The Assignment

4. The Buyer

The Property

The property in a wholesale deal can really be any type of property. I have wholesaled and bought from wholesalers land, condominiums, townhouses, manufactured homes, single-family homes, apartment buildings, office space, and even a church. Typically, a motivated seller owns these properties, someone who just doesn't want the property anymore for a number of reasons. There are several different ways to find these properties, and we will go into detail on these in a later chapter.

The Contract

The contract, or purchase contract, is a signed agreement between you and the seller stating that you will be buying the property for a certain amount of money on a certain day. Don't worry about the paperwork, I'll show you where you can get contracts later.

The Assignment

The assignment, or assignment agreement, is a signed agreement between you and the buyer stating that you are selling your interest—your rights in the contract—to them for a certain amount of money and that, by signing the agreement, they accept all of the terms within the original contract with the seller. That means that what you originally agreed to, they now have to do.

The Buyer

The buyer is the person or entity who is actually going to put up the money to buy the property. This can be a person looking for properties to fix and flip, someone looking to add to a rental portfolio or even Joe and Jane Homebuyer looking for their family home. There are different types of buyers and different reasons to go after certain ones (again, we'll cover this in more detail in a later chapter). The main thing to understand is that the buyer is the person bringing the money to the deal and they will be the eventual owner. This is how you can wholesale real estate or flip contracts with no money out of your own pocket: you aren't buying anything! Someone else, with money in their pocket, is the buyer!

Let's break this down into an actual example. You are sitting at lunch with a friend from high school who you haven't seen in a few years and explaining what you do. As you discuss your real estate-investing firm, the waiter, who has been secretly eavesdropping on your conversation, says, "Hey, if you buy houses, I need to sell mine and get out of town, do you want to buy it?" Of course, you tell him you will happily take a look at it. You ask him what the address is and how much he wants for it. He gives you the address, and tells you he just needs to get out quick and will take $130,000 for it. You let him know you will do a little research and let him know if you can help him (it's always about the seller, and it's always about helping them). While still sitting at the table, you text the address to one of your trusted realtors and ask them for an After Repair Value (ARV—this is what a house can sell for after it has been repaired or improved). Five minutes later, your realtor texts you back "ARV $190,000." As the waiter shows up to see if you are enjoying your food, you tell him "I took a look at your property and I can probably do the $130,000 on it, what kind of condition is it in?" The waiter says it's in pretty good shape, since it was remodeled before he bought it three years ago, but probably could use some new carpet and paint. You ask him for his phone number and email, and then order dessert. You text one of your repeat buyers the address and a price of $140,000, and by the time your tiramisu gets to the table, the buyer has already replied that he will take it. From your phone at the restaurant, you fill out a purchase contract and email it to the waiter for his digital signature and you send an assignment agreement to the buyer for his signature. Before the lunch bill comes to the table, you have signed contracts and $10,000 coming your way. Your friend looks across the table, smiles, and says, "You're paying for lunch."

Obviously, this is a simplified and glorified example of how this business can work, but these kinds of deals do happen and can happen that quickly. With the right team in place and a little knowledge, you can be doing deals just like this. Opportunity is out there and it is waiting for you to take action and get it.

The typical question I get when I give this is example, is "Why would this waiter sell to me?" Why? Because you offered to buy the house and solve his problem. It doesn't matter if you have never bought a house before or if you were only meeting your friend for lunch because you didn't have any money and he offered to pay for it. You can get this contract signed and write up an assignment agreement. When your buyer closes, you get the difference between the $140,000 the buyer is paying and the $130,000 the seller is getting. That is $10,000 for you!

I invited a wholesaler out for drinks with me one day. This wholesaler had been doing pretty well, I had bought six deals from him and I had paid him more than $100,000 in assignment fees in less than nine months, and I just wanted to grow our business relationship and see what I could do to help him grow his business. As we made small talk and got to know each other, I found out that he still lived with his mom, had never owned his own house, had never paid a single dollar for marketing, and he was only twenty-four years old. All of his leads were from his straight hustle. He posted free ads on Craigslist that he bought houses for cash. He posted in garage-sale groups that he could help people who were being foreclosed on. He knocked on doors and tracked down owners of vacant houses. Zero money spent on marketing. Six deals, nine months, one hundred thousand dollars. He had no education beyond books and watching free videos on YouTube. Why would people sell houses to him? He didn't have any money when he started. His car was a junker. He didn't even own his own home. Why did people sign his contracts? Because he solved their problems. You aren't really in the business of buying and selling houses, you are in the business of solving problems and helping people.

One hundred thousand dollars in profit is amazing for nine months of work, but that profit could have been over $300,000 if this wholesaler bought the houses himself, fixed them up, and flipped them. I made more than $200,000 on these deals, so why didn't he just buy them himself? Why wholesale? There are a lot of reasons to wholesale real estate instead of actually buying the property yourself, then fixing and flipping it, and for many people it is for very specific reasons. The wholesaler I mentioned above didn't want to flip because he didn't have the funds or the connection to the funds to actually purchase these houses himself. Additionally, he knew zero, zilch, nada about construction and didn't want to learn it. He had no desire to work with contractors or manage a rehab. He really just enjoyed the hunt for the property, the satisfaction of getting properties under contract, and getting the immediate reward of the assignment fee. There is nothing wrong with that. I know other people who wholesaled their first ten to twenty properties to build up some cash reserves and learn what their buyers were doing to make the projects successful flips so they in turn could find an amazing deal, buy it for themselves, get it fixed up, and then sell it and keep all the profits for themselves. They wholesale the okay deals and the decent deals but keep the best ones for themselves. This keeps their risk down and their cash flow high, as it takes money to remodel a house and sit on that property for three to nine months as it is being rehabbed and waiting to sell to a retail buyer. I know other investors who flipped houses and had so much stress from it that they just didn't want to do that side of the business anymore. Even though they were financially successful at it, they liked the quick money from wholesaling more. I know other people, like me, who just use wholesaling as another tool in their tool belts. It's easier to wholesale a property out of state, for example, than flip it in most cases. Some deals make just as much money(or more) as a wholesale deal than as a flip. It really just comes down to a numbers game and where is my money, or my private investor's money, best spent? There are many different reasons to wholesale versus fixing properties up or building your own rental portfolio. It depends on your cash flow, your desires, your comfort levels, your experience, your drive, and many other factors. Even though I fix and flip most of my own properties, I still wholesale a lot of properties as well. I've been wholesaling for years, and I will continue to wholesale in the years ahead.

The main thing to know is that there is no correct cycle to this business. You can do what you want. Some people say that you should start out wholesaling to build up funds so you can start to fix and flip. Then, as you are fixing and flipping, every five or six properties you should keep one as a rental. Once you have amassed rental properties, you should move into multifamily and apartments, and then you just become a private investor. You can do whatever you want, you don't have to follow someone else's cycle. If you want rentals, get rentals. If you don't want rentals, don't worry about them. If you want to skip single family and go straight to apartments, that is fine too. There are so many ways to make money in real estate, do what works for you. Do it honestly, do it efficiently, and repeat what works.

CASH MORE CHECKS

- This is a business, so treat it as such.

- Nobody else is going to feed your business except you.

- Success is the result of consistent and relentless action.

- Every large task is made of smaller tasks, don't get overwhelmed by the bigger picture.

- You are in the business of solving problems and helping people.

CHAPTER 2

Where Should You Start?

My goal in this book is to give you as much information as I possibly can so you can immediately get started wholesaling. Many times people get stuck waiting for the right moment, the jump start, the key thing that they have been waiting for to get them going. This probably isn't the first book on real estate investing that you have read. You've probably listened to podcasts and have probably watched videos on YouTube. You want to learn everything before you get started because you are afraid of making mistakes. Let me tell you this: you are going to make mistakes no matter how much you try to educate yourself. There will never be a more perfect time to take action than now. I don't care if you are reading this while on an airplane, in a hospital bed, or lying by a swimming pool, there are things you can do this very instant to move your wholesaling career forward. Now is the time. Yesterday would have been better. Don't wait for tomorrow, as tomorrow never comes. Right now is when you actually start.

Let's destroy some of those doubts in your mind, those self-imposed roadblocks that have kept you from taking action.

Money

Hopefully the story from the previous chapter of the wholesaler who hustled with zero dollars in marketing and made $100,000 in profit destroyed the money myth for you. You do not need money to make money in real estate. Wholesaling can be a zero-dollar business startup. If you do have money, there are a lot of things you can do with it, from buying lists, hiring virtual assistants, sending out mass mailings, creating a call center, and so much more. We'll talk about monitoring and maximizing returns in a later chapter.

Location

There are people all over the country—in fact, all over the world—in all kinds of different markets who are wholesaling. There are people in your market that are wholesaling. If they can do it, you can too. Do you have access to a phone? Do you have access to a computer (even if it is just the free one at the library—I don't want your excuses!)? You can wholesale in any market in the country. Now, I do keep saying "in the country," but that is only because I do not have experience personally in international properties, besides staying in them on vacations. But for all of my non-U.S.-based readers, I know for a fact that there are markets across the globe where other investors are doing deals for flips, wholesales, and rentals (both short and long term), and investing privately in real estate. Real estate is global, and so is the business of buying and selling houses. Each market will have its differences, but whether it is Las Vegas, Chicago, Brisbane, or Obidos, there most likely is a way to make money in real estate. If I can wholesale or flip a property 2,325 miles away (the distance between Las Vegas, Nevada, and Tampa, Florida), what's the difference of another mile or another five thousand miles? You can do this business anywhere. In fact, while on vacation in Florence, Italy, last summer I closed nine deals, that's 5,977 miles (9,619 kilometers). So the excuse of a property being thirty minutes or even three hours away through heavy traffic does not work. If you make that excuse, you are hindering yourself. Realize it and stop it. If other people are working deals from across the globe, you can do it from across town. Whether you are wholesaling locally or wholesaling virtually, your location is always a benefit.

Market Cycles

Perhaps you don't think your market is ripe for wholesaling because of the economy. You are wrong, there are always ways to wholesale properties. In a hot market, an upward market where people say it is too hard to find a deal, you can still find deals and that will be the easiest market to sell a house in. You will have buyers lining up and fighting for your properties. In a stable market, people are still buying houses, still moving and, even though it is less competitive, you will be able to buy properties for less and still be able to sell them. Downward markets are prime for buying properties. When markets are in a free fall, some people are looking to run and get out, but others are looking to run and get in. This is where people (and investment firms) are looking to amass rental portfolios. They know the market will eventually go back up, so they can buy now at cheap prices, rent out properties and, when the market goes up, they increase in value. Having a mix of flippers, landlords, and retail buyers is how you combat the market cycles. Up markets, down markets, stable markets, it doesn't matter. No matter the market conditions, you can wholesale properties.

Contracts And Forms

You've never written a contract before? You can't pay a lawyer to help you? What if the paperwork is wrong? These are all excuses. I am going to give you the actual purchase contract and the actual assignment contract that I use in my business. Now each market is different, and you can spend thousands and thousands on lawyers to write and rewrite contracts specific to your market (a lawyer doesn't like a contract he didn't write). Where else can you find contracts and forms? You can find all sorts of items, both good and bad, on the internet. I am not a lawyer, I am not a legal expert, but I like my contracts and I close deals with them in multiple states. When we dig into the forms, we'll talk about understanding some of the nuances of contracts and how I deal with them, and how you can actually get free help in your market. Contracts and forms are nothing to be afraid of.

Time

I don't have enough time to call them back. I don't have time to drive neighborhoods looking for empty houses. I'm too busy with my kid's school. I'm too busy with my job. I'm too busy. There's not enough time in the day. I just couldn't get to it. Lies. Lies. Lies. You are lying to yourself if this is what you are saying. You and I have the same amount of time in the day. You just aren't using your time to its highest potential. Are you going after instant gratification versus long-term satisfaction? Are you binge watching shows on Netflix and Hulu? Are you playing video games? Are you sleeping in on weekends? Are you trolling social media on your phone while you sit on the toilet? Your time is controlled by your choices. If you want to be successful at anything, you have to choose to use your time wisely and to its fullest potential. Habits can be broken, cycles can be changed, and it all comes down to choice. I choose to be successful. What do you choose? Cancel your cable and streaming services, remove the time-suck apps from your phone, sell your Xbox or Playstation. Get off your ass and take action! You, me, and Elon Musk all have the same amount of time in the day. What you do with it will determine your level of success.

There are so many reasons why people will say they can't do something. I am not a fan of excuses, of "can't". While I have an abundance mentality, I also have a positive mindset. I surround myself with positive people, positive music, positive reading, and my own positive thoughts. This is something you have to train yourself for. Just like getting rid of the distractions, you may have to get rid of negative people in your life. Don't let other people tell you that you can't. I know you can do this business. Anybody can do this business. I know wholesalers who are in high school, I know wholesalers who were born into real estate, I know wholesalers who are ex-felons, I know wholesalers who never graduated high school, and I know wholesalers with three master's degrees. This industry is an equal opportunity employer, everyone is welcome!

So where do you start? That is the title of this chapter. You start in your mind, you start on your front door, your start in your local market, you start virtually, you just have to start. But you need to start with focused action and to do that you need to know what you need. In Chapter 1, I explained the four main parts of a wholesale deal: the property, the contract, the assignment, and the buyer. That is where your focused action is going to be. Since I am going to give you a purchase contract and an assignment agreement, the remaining things you need to focus on are properties and buyers. There is some debate about what you should concentrate on first, finding buyers or finding properties, but I say they are both right. You need both to do a deal, so spend time finding both right away. It's like asking should I buy a carriage or a horse first? Or, as my son recently asked me, should I buy the monitor or the Xbox first? Either way, you need both!

Here is what you need to do right now. And when I write "now," I mean now. I am going to tell you to do something, I want you to put this book down and do it. How many authors actually tell you to put a book down? I do, and I am serious about it. I did the same thing in *The Flipping Blueprint* and there are people all over the country having amazing results. Here is your first thing you need to do, step by step:

1. Go to Craigslist, search for your city-specific Craigslist (or the largest metro area near you).

2. Click on "Post to Classifieds"—select "Housing Offered"—select "real estate—by owner"

3. Now fill out the form. I like to make the title something that will grab the attention of potential buyers. Here are a couple of examples: "Property needs work, perfect for a flip," "Tired landlord ready to sell rentals quick," "Water damaged property, wholesale deal."

4. For the specific location field, just put the name of the metro area you are using. If you are using St. Louis, write St. Louis, don't write Glendale.

5. Add in a zip code. If you are in a market you are unfamiliar with, search for zip code map images and just pick a zip code from that map.

6. For the posting body, keep it simple. "Property has been vacant for a couple years, has some water damage. Looking for serious buyers only, cash only. Send me your contact info and I will call you to discuss. Send phone and email or I won't reply to you."

7. Now here is the part that will drive responses the most. Open a new browser window, go to Bing, and look up "real estate xxxxx" (don't type actual xs, type your zip code). The reason why you go to Bing is the way the results are shown. You will get a list of five properties with prices and square footage. Take whatever property is the middle value. Use that square footage and put it in the square footage field on your Craigslist post. Whatever price that house is listed for on Bing, divide that price in half and put that as your price on Craigslist.

8. Housing type = house

9. Laundry = w/d in unit

10. Parking = attached garage

11. Bedrooms = 3

12. Bathrooms = 2

13. Available on = today

14. Type your email into the two fields and make sure to use the "CL mail relay," this way your email isn't

shown to people looking at the ad and Craigslist will just forward all of the emails from their contact. Skip the next fields for phone number and property-specific address and click on "Continue." Also click "Continue" on the map page.

15. Ads with an image get more responses, so add an image. Go back to Bing and search for an image that goes with the title and comments for your ad. If you mentioned water damage, search for "Water damaged house," for example. It shouldn't take twenty minutes to find a perfect image. Spend one minute, find an image, and save it to your desktop. Go back to your Craigslist posting, click on the "Add image" button, find the image you just saved on your desktop, and then click "Done with Images."

16. Click the "Publish" button. Now, most markets will send an email to the email address you listed on the ad to make sure everything works. Go into your email, find the email from Craigslist, click on the link provided, read and accept the terms of use, and now your post is active!

So, what is this that you really did? You don't actually have this house for sale or any house at all ... yet. This is what some people call a ghost ad, a teaser ad, or just a lead-generating ad. In the real estate wholesaling world, this has become pretty common practice, whether you post an ad like this on Craigslist or even on Facebook group pages. It is a quick, easy, and free way to start building your potential buyers list. You posted about a property that sounds too good to be true, remember? You put it at half the price other houses are selling for. So who will actually respond? Potential buyers will respond to this ad, some will provide the information requested, others will just send out a one-line email saying "send me the address" with no name, phone number, or any other way to contact them besides the Craigslist relay email. Every response is a good response. Be prepared, as there will be plenty of people who respond that are not real buyers, perhaps they are other wholesalers, or perhaps they are new to the industry and don't understand the actual nature of this ad. As you get responses, keep a spreadsheet of who responds to you. Name, company name, phone number, email, and what they do. Put several ads up over this next week and regularly from then on, as there are always new buyers entering the market. Additionally, be prepared, because people will flag your posts on Craigslist, as they fear competition. Remember, we have an abundance mentality. Don't flag other people's posts, there are enough deals for everyone.

Not all buyers are on Craigslist, in fact, maybe only five to ten percent of them are, but it is a good place to start. We'll dig into buyers in more depth in a later chapter, but I wanted you to see that you can get started immediately in this business. Now, if you are one of those people who is just reading and hasn't stopped and taken action as I described above, this is me telling you again, stop what you are doing and go back and place an ad now. Get the ball rolling. No excuses. You can do this from your phone or any computer out there. If you aren't willing to do this, what else are you not willing to do? Don't let your head get in the way of your success!

Lots of people spend so much time doing busy work that they never actually do the real work. Here is a list of busy work items that I recommend you do or get, but don't let these get in the way of your actual work of finding properties and finding buyers. These can overall help you with getting more leads and closing more deals, but are not actually necessary!

Create a Limited Liability Corporation (a LLC). LLCs are great in my opinion, as they allow you to capture business expenses and use those against profits for tax advantages (I'm not a tax expert, so don't ask me the specifics on how this all works, I just know that it does). As you make more money, you will have to pay more taxes. I've seen gurus push this type of busy work so hard they have students with five or six LLCs, a trust, and multiple business aliases at the cost of thousands and thousands of dollars, but their student hasn't even done one deal. Why do some of these people push this so hard? Because they make commission from it. LLCs are great, most people should get one if you are doing business. If you haven't done any business yet, it can wait. Again, I am neither a lawyer nor a tax consultant, so if you need legal or tax advice, find an independent expert to help you with that. I can tell you that, in my experience, most wholesalers have one LLC and do just fine with that.

Business Cards. Don't over think business cards, they just need your name, phone number, email address, and to tell people what you do. When I first started, I purposefully designed my cards to stand out. I went to events and everyone else's cards all looked the same. A picture of them or a logo made on Fiverr, lots of words and contact information, but it never simply said what they did. My cards were a single color. I had a bright red one and an all black one. The front had my name, company name (my LLC), phone number, and email. On the back it said the following:

I BUY HOUSES

Quick Close, No Fees

Any Condition

Call me for a NO-OBLIGATION Cash Offer

Simple, easy, and straight forward. You have to understand who you want to actually reach with business cards. If you are handing your cards out to other investors at meetings or real estate events, they will understand what you do, so you don't really need to direct market to them. With business cards, you are marketing to potential sellers and that is who your message should be speaking to. Any type of marketing you do, and a business card is marketing, should be done with purpose. What is the hook to bring in a potential seller? Why would they contact you? If you have a stack of business cards, which one is going to stand out the most, another white or blue one with a logo and some fancy tag line and a whole lot of nothing? Or will the bright green one in the middle of the stack with the simple but straight-forward wording be the one you gravitate to? Keep it simple and don't over think it. Thicker card stock is better, pay for that upgrade and order some cards.

Websites and Domain Names. I am a fan of people getting their own domain name, their own web address. That way they don't have to use a Gmail or yahoo email address. You can use a custom email like <u>Simon@SimonBuysHouses.com</u> or maybe something more generic like <u>Offers@cash4anyhome.com</u> (if one of these is your actual email, kudos to you! I just made them up while typing this) and it does give you a bit more legitimacy in the eyes of a seller than other potential buyers out there. Notice the names I choose. It's not city or state specific, because this business is not city or state specific. I've done deals all across the country, so set your business up to allow you to do that. When potential sellers go to my website, they don't know that I am not located right next door to them. Domains can be bought for around ten dollars a year on sites like GoDaddy, and even Gmail and Yahoo! have their own services that will easily link to your existing email accounts. As for websites, there are a lot of different services out there that can build and customize websites. I use OnCarrot or Investor Carrot for some of my websites. They are simple and easy to use, already come with content, and can help you manage lead generation as well. Don't try to build something from scratch to start. Remember, this is busy work at the beginning and as you add more of these services into your business, you are adding expenses.

Social Media. Social media is not just busy work, it is a time-sucking demon that can destroy your business! In *The Flipping Blueprint*, I recommend people use a good old-fashioned kitchen egg timer, one where you can hear the click-click-click of the seconds going by. You don't want to lose hours of your day looking at what other people are doing. Do social media with purpose, a plan, and a set time frame. Five minutes, twenty minutes, sixty minutes, but with set objectives to accomplish within that period. Create your business, don't live through the dreams of other people's postings. You can easily create a free business page on Facebook and create a free Instagram account to go with your business. There are lots of different ways to show legitimacy on these. Post pictures and content. But again, like the business card, do this with purpose in mind. Put the hook on everything, "contact me today for your no-obligation cash offer," or "Do you need to sell your house, but don't want to pay real estate commissions? Contact me today, never a commission to pay!" Don't just post a picture of a house and say, "Look at this dump." Post the picture and say, "We bought this house. If yours looks like this (better or worse), we'll buy it too!" Additionally, reviews and testimonials are great. If your mom says "If I had two houses I would sell both of them to Brian! He is wonderful," that's a review you can post! Just don't give credit from "–my mom", give the credit to "–Jayne from Tacoma." Simple marketing tricks go a long way. Although this is still busy work, it does help with the future foundation of your business.

Learning. Yes, this one may seem out of place here, but I have been told hundreds, if not thousands, of times that people get so wrapped up in trying to learn everything that they never end up doing anything and learning just becomes busy work. "I have to listen to this podcast," "I have to read this blog," "I have to watch these videos." What you have to do is get up, get moving, and get doing! The best way to learn is by doing things. If this is the fifth book you are reading on wholesaling and you haven't done a deal yet, it's not because you don't have the knowledge base it's because you are not getting out there and looking at enough properties and making enough offers! That being said, I still read, I still listen to podcasts, and I still network, but I don't let that get in the way of my needed business activities. I would be a bit of a hypocrite if I said don't read books at all as you are reading this book and I wrote it. But you probably get my point by now.

Networking Events and Real Estate Investment Associations (REIAs). I actually have grown to love networking events, so much so that I throw my own events both in Vegas and in other cities when I travel. However, there are some people who I see every time, and they complain about not having the time or energy to find properties to wholesale. If you aren't finding properties, what are you networking for? There typically aren't private sellers at these types of events. Now don't get me wrong, everyone needs a break once in a while, moral support and good education is great. But when you go to every event in town, every meet up that costs twenty dollars so they can pitch someone else's product to you, you are probably wasting your time and this is just empty busy work. If you have already met buyers at a few of these events, no need to go to the next one. Spend the two or four hours you would have spent getting dressed, driving to the event, and sitting in a chair listening to a sales pitch and instead cold call potential sellers; walk a neighborhood, door knocking and leaving door hangers; call expired listings; stuff envelopes; or one of many other productive activities to find those deals.

Some of this busy work is necessary items that you will need to do for your business to grow, but they don't all have to be done at once and they aren't necessary to finding deals and wholesaling properties. Time management is a hard task to learn for many people, but awareness is the first step to managing it. Time block your activities, which means, set an alarm and write up a calendar of what you are going to do for the next three hours in twenty-minute increments. You will see your productivity increase dramatically when you go into something with a plan. You don't have a boss looking over your shoulder anymore telling you what to do and when to do it. This is your business. Time is your most valuable resource, don't squander it.

CASH MORE CHECKS

- This business can be done anywhere.

- No excuses, don't limit yourself.

- Tomorrow will never come, get started today!

- Market with purpose, always have a hook.

- Time block your activities.

- Time is your most valuable resource, don't squander it.

CHAPTER 3

Build Your Lead-Generating
Machine—No to Low Cost

I can't even tell you how many times I have been asked the question "Where do you find your leads?" The simple answer to this is "Everywhere." There are so many different lead sources and ways to find leads it's crazy, in my opinion, to focus on just one. Most wholesalers have a primary lead source. This is the channel that brings in the most leads to your company, and what it is will really depend on you. It will depend on your marketing budget, it will depend on your sales ability, it will depend on how well you take rejection (there is a lot of rejection in the wholesaling game), and so on. The most important thing you can do is track your leads. It doesn't have to be some fancy program or an overly complicated method, but you do want to track your leads to make sure you are spending the time, energy, and money on your highest-performing lead generators.

Let's dig into the various forms of lead generation. We will go from the cheapest to some of the most expensive. Keep in mind, a lot of these lead-generating tips will bring in not just sellers but will also help connect you with potential buyers too.

Social Media Posting

This can be a zero-dollar lead source. You can set up multiple Instagram, TikTok, Twitter, and Facebook accounts for you, your business, and your websites, and you plaster everywhere that you pay cash for houses. Each account should be posting three to four times a week with unique content. Here are multiple items you can post:

1. Pictures of ugly houses saying you will buy any house, any condition.

2. Before and after pictures (these get a lot of attention).

3. Short videos about how you help solve issues for homeowners.

4. Walk-throughs of properties in good and bad shape. Keep these videos to less than one minute and make sure to have a hook at the end, something like "Contact me today to receive your no obligation cash offer."

5. Funny memes. Break up the sales pitches with some humorous postings. Maybe pick one day a week to post a joke.

6. Ask questions to get more interaction. These should be questions like:

    a. Do you want to sell your house fast?

b. Do you know how to sell your house with zero fees?

c. Is your house not selling as fast as you thought it would?

d. Do you have problem tenants?

e. Are you tired of fixing someone else's toilet?

f. Do you need money to fix a roof? Why fix it at all?

g. Are you behind on your mortgage?

h. Is your house too small for your family?

i. Do you hate your neighbors?

j. Are you behind on your property taxes?

7. Pictures of title and escrow companies, with a statement about how you just helped out another family by buying their house and solving their problems by putting a check in their pocket.

8. Pictures of you with sellers at a house along with their review of you (video testimonials are great).

Notice that nowhere in here am I telling you to post pictures of cars, checks, or motivational quotes. How are any of those going to tell a seller you want to offer them money for their house? I said it in *The Flipping Blueprint*, and I am saying it here again, do this with purpose. Do you think a seller is going to sell to you after you post a check saying you made $30,000 on a wholesale fee? No. Do you think a seller is going to sell to you after you post pictures of your dream car five days in a row? No. Do you think a seller will sell to you if they see posts of you helping other sellers? Yes. Do you think a seller is going to sell to you if they see before and after pictures of properties you bought (or at least got under contract and wholesaled, but then make it look like you did the rehab by getting the after photos from your end buyer—yes, you can do that)? Yes. This is all free marketing for you. Posting pictures, stories, and questions will get attention, but make sure you are posting to get the right attention. Post with purpose!

You can turn your social media into a low- or a high-cost lead-source tool by placing paid ads on social media. Typically, wholesalers will spend their money on Facebook and Instagram. You can hire professionals to do this for you as well. We'll talk more about this as an additional and possibly more expensive tool in the next chapter.

Driving For Dollars

While writing this book, I actually received a phone call from someone wanting to buy one of the houses that I am flipping, not wholesaling. This is what you should not do when driving for dollars (D4D). This guy, let's call him Boyd, called me and said, "I'm calling about the house on Flamingo. What's the status with that?" That was his opening line, there was no introduction and no prior communication. I had no idea who this guy was or why he was calling my personal cell phone. I asked him who he was and he told me his name was Boyd and he buys houses. I wanted to find out how he got my personal cell number, as I don't post that in places that are easy to find. He told me that he drove by my property (which my LLC owns and my LLC is shown as the owner in the tax records), and it looked a little run down, so he searched on the internet and found my cell phone number and then called me.

I asked him if he saw our sign in the front yard, as we post our own "We pay cash for houses" signs in the front yard of all of our flips with our business phone number. He said yes, he saw it (I didn't ask him why he didn't just call that number instead). I then asked him "What are you wanting to know about the house?" because, hey, you never know when someone may be a potential business connection or even a buyer or a seller. He asked me if it was for sale and I told him it would be once we were done with our remodel on it. He told me that's what his company does as well, and he was already trying to get me off the phone at this point. I then proceeded to tell him (nicely) to not spend his time calling companies who have purchased a house in the past twelve months, he's better off spending his time calling individuals who have owned a house for more than a year. If you are going to spend time, and possibly money, skip-tracing someone (skip-tracing is the process of going through available records, either physical or online, to find contact information for an owner of a property, either a company or a trust, and there are paid services out there that will do this for you), make sure you are going after the right people. Yes, I scolded him a bit and he just wanted to get off the phone, but hopefully he learned something and is more successful in his real-estate investing because of it! And who knows, maybe someday I will wholesale him a property, as I did enter his information into my buyer database.

What should Boyd have done? Let's play through this example two different ways.

Scenario One: Boyd is out driving for dollars and comes across a property on Flamingo. He notices there is some roof damage, weeds growing in the front yard, and the blinds in the windows look damaged and are missing in some spots. He takes several pictures of the house and writes down the address in his notepad as one to follow up on. When he gets back home, he searches the address on the local county assessor/appraiser website and finds the owner is XYZ, LLC, and they bought the property two months ago for what appears to be a low price. This most likely is a flipper or a landlord looking for more properties. Boyd does a search in the county records and finds XYZ, LLC owns more than sixty houses, with a mix of recent purchases as well as a couple of dozen properties they have owned for more than two years. This looks like someone Boyd should know. XYZ buys a decent number of houses and it appears they may do both rentals and flips. Boyd continues his research and finds a phone number from a couple of Google searches and calls, eventually reaching someone at the company. When they answer, he begins the conversation with "Hi. My name is Boyd. I saw that your company owns a property at 123 Flamingo Avenue. Are you looking for more properties in that area to buy?" (Give the person a chance to reply) "I get a couple properties a month under contract in that area, and was wondering if you would be interested in them?" So what did Boyd do? He turned what he was hoping to be a purchase into a potential proven buyer for his next deals. He gets the appropriate phone number and an email address and contact name from the person he is talking to and adds them into his buyer list.

Scenario 2: Boyd is out driving for dollars and comes across a property on Flamingo. He notices there is some roof damage, weeds growing in the front yard, and the blinds in the windows look damaged and are missing in some spots. He takes several pictures of the house and writes down the address in his notepad as one to follow up on. When he gets back home, he searches the address on the local county assessor/appraiser website and finds the seller is Bob and Marie Bartowski and they bought the property twelve years ago. Now in Boyd's particular county, it even shows the mailing address for the owner and it shows they live in a completely different state. Additionally, the local county website shows that the property taxes are up to date. The house is damaged and looks empty, there is an out-of-state owner, and they are paying the bills on the house, which means it is costing the owners money. This is a great potential deal with multiple sales tactics to go after. Boyd skip-traces the owner, finds someone on Facebook with the same name and in the same state as the mailing address, and sends them a private message on Facebook. "It looks like you are the owner of a property on Flamingo in Anytown. If you are connected to this property, please contact me, as I have something I need to discuss regarding the condition of it." Make sure to provide your phone and email in the message. Does Boyd stop there? No. He mails a letter to the mailing address on record that states he buys houses and came across the property on Flamingo and wanted to know if the owner was interested in receiving a no-obligation cash offer for the property. The letter that he mails also has a picture of the house, taking up one-third of the page, making sure that enough detail is there to show some of the damage that the owner may not even be aware of. Boyd continues to skip-trace the owner himself and finds four different phone numbers potentially associated with the owner of record. He calls the first one, and the person tells him he doesn't own any property in that state and hangs up. The second one tells him to take a hike. The third one says, "Yes, I own that property, why are you calling me?" At this point, Boyd asks if the seller would be interested in selling the property to him and he goes through his sales pitch (we'll talk more about that later). The seller is interested, and Boyd schedules an appointment with the seller to walk the property and present an offer. What does Boyd do with the fourth number? Nothing! He's already found the owner.

While driving for dollars, there are a few additional things you can do. If you find a potential property, stop the car, and knock on the door to see if anyone is home. If no one is home, leave a door hanger on the knob and a business card in the crack in the door. The door hangars we use have "Confidential" written on the outside in big bold letters, and a letter with a business card inside the envelope.

In this scenario, you can use multiple approaches at the same time to get a deal. How many did we use? D4D, door knocking, door hangers, skip tracing, mailers, cold calling, and social media contacts. How much did this lead cost? A couple dollars in fuel, a couple pieces of paper, an envelope and stamp, a door hangar, and a couple of business cards. All in, you may have five dollars into this lead and a few hours of your time. Most people in this business only use one of these methods, but the more thorough you are on each lead, the higher chance of success you have. How do you become successful in the business of wholesaling? Be better than the rest!

Here are some key features you want to look for when driving for dollars:

- Damaged roofs

- Overgrown lawns (think months of no mowing, not just a week or two)

- Damaged blinds in windows, or a mix of blinds, drapes, and so on

- Trash in the yard (front, sides, or back)

- Broken windows

- Window or wall air conditioners when these are not common in the area

- Holiday decorations still up months after the holiday

- Notices taped to the front doors (these are usually eviction or auction notices)

- Broken-down cars (especially if they have parking enforcement stickers on the window)

- For Sale By Owner signs (this one should be obvious)

- For Rent signs (if there is a sign in front, it's typically vacant and the owner is losing money)

Each market will have some different nuances that will help you know if a house is vacant, too. Maybe in the winter you notice that a house never has the snow shoveled or there are no tire tracks in the driveway. Perhaps as you drive by a house in the evening you see it never has lights on. Maybe on trash day, the garbage cans are never put out. A house doesn't have to look bad to be a potential for driving for dollars, it could just be vacant. Keep your eyes open, these houses are everywhere.

Door Knocking

When I think of salesmen, this is really what comes to mind. Someone walking from door to door in a neighborhood, up one street and down the next, knocking on every single door, and selling. This is the door-to-door vacuum-cleaner-seller approach. This really is the beginning of the thick-skin sale approaches. You will get a lot of rejection, probably some threats (imagine the cartoon image of an old man shaking his fist yelling "Get off my lawn" and then he goes inside to get his shotgun), dogs barking, strange invitations, and either very short or very long conversations.

Be aware, this approach is truly an art form, as you have to sell yourself multiple times to this person. You have to sell yourself to just get in the doors to these houses. Let me try to paint this picture a little better for you. You target a zip code, an area of older homes where cash buyers are purchasing houses to fix and flip. You park your car at the end of one street, you are dressed nicely enough, but not too nice (think polo shirt and clean pants and shoes), you have a backpack or satchel holding some paperwork, and you start walking the street. The first couple of houses look like they are well taken care of, the lawn is clean, there are nice drapes in the window, and they even look like they could have been recently flipped since they have fresh exterior paint, a newer front door, and newer light fixtures.

The third house you get to is just okay looking. The front porch light is a sconce that is missing its top cap and is slightly crooked. The front door is dented a bit and you can see a mix of blinds, curtains, and possibly a blanket being used as window coverings. The roof looks okay except for a couple missing shingles. This is your target. You open the front gate, go up the walkway to the front door, and immediately hear a dog barking. As you get closer to the front porch, you see the blinds shaking on the window, but you're not sure if it is the owner or the dog eyeing you to see who is trespassing on the lawn. You climb the three wooden steps of the front porch, and the handrail almost falls off as you accidentally put too much weight on it.

As you reach the front door, you hear someone yell at the dog and the barking stops. Someone is definitely home. You press the doorbell, but nothing happens. Did it ring? Should you press it again? You don't want to be too bossy and annoying, so you wait ten seconds, slowly counting in your head and this time, as you press the button you listen a little more intently, leaning in toward the door. Definitely no chimes coming from the inside. You wait another five grueling seconds and then knock on the front door, loud enough to be heard but not so loud to be rude. Another ten seconds go by and, as you reach your fist up to knock one more time, the door swings open. An older man appears in the doorway, wearing just a pair of shorts and no shirt, with television noise in the background. He's dressed as if he wasn't expecting anyone, because, well, he wasn't. He looks at you and says, "Can I help you?" and it's not in the friendliest tone. This is where it starts. What do you say? How is he going to react? Where did the dog go? This is what I say.

"Hi, my name is Luke. Sorry to disturb you, but I am walking the neighborhood and talking to homeowners about putting money in their pockets. Are you the owner of this property?

"Yeah, I own it. What are you selling?"

"Actually, I am not selling anything. I'm buying. Actually, the company I work for is buying. They are buying houses in this neighborhood, paying cash, and closing within the seller's time frame. Is that something you would be interested in?"

"How much are you offering?"

"Right now I am actually just making contact with interested sellers, so I can't make you an offer on your doorstep right now. I wouldn't want to make an offer too low and without knowing a little more about your house. If you are interested, I could come in, take a look around, take some pictures, it'll only take a couple minutes.

"Alright, just give me a second"

The owner closes the door and, about a minute later, he comes back to the door, shirt on, television off, and tells you to come on in. This is where your sales skills really start to come into play. You've already had to sell yourself right on the front step, everything you do from the moment you step onto the sidewalk in front of the house you have to assume is being watched. Walk straight and upright, don't be on your phone on their porch, and ring the doorbell or knock with confidence. Smile, but not too much. Be personable and pleasant, even when they are not. Remember, you are the one showing up uninvited. These are blind, no-appointment interruptions at someone's place of safety, their home where they raise and protect their kids, their retreat from the grind of their jobs, and you are an intruder. Respect them and the situation, but also go into it knowing that you belong there as well. Treat them like you are a distant cousin and find some ground of commonality. "I watch that show, too." "I saw your Mustang out front, that's a nice car, my dad had one." "I love your dress." Find some commonality, but don't dwell on it and try to stay on point. Keep it small talk and let them talk, but don't keep adding to subjects or taking the conversation on different tangents. If they say they have been to Paris, you can say that you have always wanted to go. Don't say, you've always wanted to go, but the closest you ever made it was to the Paris Casino in Las Vegas, because you'll end up having a thirty-minute conversation about Las Vegas. Stay on point, you are there to buy a house.

Additionally, one thing I don't like to do is point out the negative qualities of the house. Smells, water damage, or a poorly kept lawn, don't focus on these when you are with the seller. It's their home, they know what works or doesn't work, but it is theirs and you don't want to insult it or them. What you want to do is focus on what they would do with the money. Do you want to go back to Paris? Where else would you travel? Would you like to be able to get an engine back into the Mustang? No matter how friendly, unfriendly, or off topic you get, you have to take it back to the sale, and the sale will only happen if you find some sort of motivation of the seller and tap into it.

On these initial inspections, unless you have done your research on the houses beforehand, you won't be making an offer, you'll be getting photos—a lot of photos, at least one hundred. I tell my inspectors to get at least two pictures of each room and each exterior side of the house and roof and, additionally, get multiple pictures of any problems they find in the house as well as any positive things in the house. Does the house have good tile or wood flooring? Get a couple pictures of it. If the tile is cracked or the wood is all scratched up from the dogs, get pictures of that. Get pictures of all the mechanicals, the water heater, the air conditioner, the furnace, and the electrical panel. Get pictures of under sinks and inside showers. Why do you need so many pictures? Because your buyers will want them, and this way you don't have to go back to the house and disturb the seller. Notice how I keep saying seller and not owner? Change your mindset on these people and start believing they are sellers. That will show in your interactions with them, and help turn them into actual sellers.

To finish the inspection, I usually ask a couple questions:

- "How's everything working in the house? Water heater, heat and air conditioning?

- "How quickly would you want to move if we can come to an agreement on price? That way we know what to write in the offer when we send it to you.

At this point, one of two things will happen. If you haven't done any research on the property value, you'll let them know that either you or one of your co-workers will reach out to them (make sure to get their full contact info: name, phone numbers, and email) with an offer in the next twenty-four hours. Thank them for allowing you to enter the house (I don't like to use the word home with sellers, as I want to get them away from the mindset of the property being a home. Remove the emotional attachment for them by using the terms the property or the house in the conversation instead of your home). Also, make sure to leave them your contact information, a business card is great, or if you just have your own printed brochure or material, as long as they can reach you and remember you. Finally, I like to shake people's hands. A firm (but not too firm) handshake and looking people in the eyes with a smile gives the sensation of conclusion. That is a good feeling to leave people with. As you leave, remember, you are probably still being watched. Go on to the next house, and the next one. Hit up a couple more properties and, once you have gotten inside your target number of homes for the day (five is a good number), get back to your computer and start running numbers, because you have offers to make.

Now, if you already ran your numbers—perhaps you were doing selective door knocking off of a list you had already made while driving for dollars or a pre-foreclosure list you bought, this is when you ask the seller, "Is it okay if we sit down and I can explain the process?" I like to do this while in the kitchen, and I'll point to the table or a breakfast bar. It's best to sit eye level to eye level, that way it is a conversation between equals versus one of you sitting or standing at a higher level and having an overbearing or superior position.

Everyone is going to have different sales tactics, and you have to do what feels right to you and you are comfortable with. Sales really is a personality business. Some people strong arm, some people go soft, some people lie or make false promises (don't do that), some people talk a lot, other people talk very little, but you are going to have to find the approach that works best for you and that will take experience. Additionally, I recommend getting some training in sales. There are a lot of different programs, and they don't have to be real-estate specific at all. The best sales programs work no matter what the industry, because they are teaching you how to read people and situations, how to turn a no into a maybe and a maybe into a yes. They will teach you how to be comfortable and confident. When you are investing in your business in the early stages, sales training is a great place to start. All of that being said, I'll tell you the approach that works for me.

Sitting at the kitchen table, I don't get into big stories and recap their house. At this point, they are waiting for the number and not really listening to you until they hear that number. This is my typical sales pitch.

"After walking the house, I can offer you $120,000 That is a net number to you, meaning we will pay all the closing costs and fees associated with the closing. There are no commissions paid, and we'll take the property in its current condition, meaning no repairs need to be made. We really like to make this the easiest real estate transaction you've ever had." Chances are, they had issues with prior transactions, it's just the way it goes. Additionally, I like to offer a price that has wiggle room. I don't make my highest offer right then and there. I want them to have the ability to win also, even if it is just a moral victory of getting the price up $2,000 on the initial offer. You shouldn't defend or justify your offer after you give it to them. They don't care about the house down the street that sold for $112,000, they only care about their house. Make your offer and wait. Wait for them to ask questions, to say no, to say yes, to say that they need to think about it. Sit there and wait for them to say something.

When they try to negotiate, I let them know that, "We really like to make our best offer the first time, remember, I'm trying to make this the easiest possible for you." These conversations can go a lot of different ways at this point. You may leave a contract with them. They may just tell you to get out. They may take your offer and want to sign on the spot. If they decline the offer, find out why and ask them how much they were expecting. If you don't get the offer signed right then and there, make sure to leave the door open. "I'll get back to my office and see if we can do anything about the number." Leave a way for you to come back and offer more, or offer more over the phone. I do use the word "We" and so should you, even if you are only a one-person operation, the seller won't know that. Say we, and let them know you'll need to talk to your partner and get back to them. Above all, just remember that every "No" is one step closer to a "Yes."

Pretty good, you got into the first house you tried. You got to the table and were able to make an offer. Chances are, you are going to not get into eighty to ninety percent of the doors you knock on. Either people won't be home, they aren't interested in selling, or they aren't the owners. Don't just walk away from the people you talk to because they aren't interested. Make sure to ask them these two questions.

1. "Do you know anyone who might be interested in selling?"

2. "Are there any problem properties in the neighborhood you would like to see us buy and fix up?"

These two questions can get you a lot more free leads. All it took was a little bit of your time. Remember, the more people who know what you do and the more people you talk to, the more houses you will get under contract.

Door Hangars

What do you do with all those houses where you knock on the doors and no one answers? I leave door hangars. This is an envelope that you can slip over a doorknob so it will hang there and not blow away in the wind. The version I use has a sealed envelope compartment and I place a very simple letter in it. The letter opens with a question, then has several statements:

- Are you interested in selling your house?

- We pay cash for houses and never charge commissions or real estate fees.

- Close on your schedule and even stay in the home after you have sold.

- Call today for your no-obligation cash offer.

- Your name, phone number, and email address.

I also like to include a business card inside the envelope as well. When they open the envelope, the business card usually slides out onto the floor, they have to pick it up and look at it, and they look at the letter. It's two immediate touches in one sitting. Additionally, people are more prone to keep a business card then a letter. I get leads from door hangars. If people aren't opening their doors when you knock, at least let them know you were there and why you were there.

For Sale By Owner

For Sale by Owners (FSBO) are a great source of free leads. The great thing about technology is that it has made it so much easier to find these. You use to have to drive neighborhoods looking for the signs in the front yards or search the Sunday newspaper real estate section. Now there are dozens of websites people can post their houses on for free. Here is a list of websites we get free FSBO leads from:

- www.ForSaleByOwner.com

- www.FSBO.com

- www.Owners.com

- www.4SaleByOwner.com

- www.Fizber.com

- www.Zillow.com

- www.Redfin.com

- www.Craigslist.com

- www.ByOwner.com

- www.HelpUSell.com

Some of these even offer limited multiple listing services (MLS) or other real estate-related services to owners. These sites alone can give you enough leads in some markets to keep your pipeline full. Using these as a lead source, in combination with door knocking, cold calling (many of these sites have phone numbers and email contact for the sellers), and door hangars, is a business model to itself for many wholesalers. On these, though, time is of the essence. You want to be the first one in the door making the offer. These sellers don't always know what their home is worth or they just need to sell. Get in contact with them and get them an offer as soon as possible.

This is a business model for other wholesalers, so act fast, because if you don't someone else will. When I first got into real estate, I spent a lot of time with FSBOs. I found it a great way to hone my sales skills. Think about it. They are a willing audience; they want to listen to your pitch. You already know they want to sell, it's just about getting them at your price. You should be calling every single FSBO and getting in the door. The best way to learn is through experience. Who knows? You might just get your first deal because of this!

Expired Listings

Expired listings are another great way to find a willing audience. These are sellers you already know want to sell, they have been on market with a Realtor and they just couldn't sell. Most of the time, it is because their price was too high. If they were listed at $350,000, reduced the price to $320,000 after forty-five days, and still sat on the market for another seventy-five days with no sale occurring, you can be pretty sure the property is not worth $320,000. Your main competition for expired listings typically isn't other wholesalers, it's real estate agents. This is a great source of leads for agents, they typically have the seller's contact information from the previous listing information, and they will be calling that seller directly. I've actually experienced this. Every once in a while, I have one of my flips that doesn't sell as fast as I planned and the listing expires. I get ten to twenty calls a day from Realtors offering to list my property for me, but rarely do I get someone offering me cash for my house. To get a list of expired listings, you'll want to collaborate with a Realtor who will just email you a list from the MLS, which is a database Realtors use to list properties.

I get a better response in my market when I mail expired listings my cash-offer letter. If they are getting ten to twenty calls a day, they probably have stopped answering their phone. The day a listing expires, I send them a letter with the following verbiage:

- I saw you recently listed your house for sale and it did not sell. If you are still interested in selling your house, I'd like to make you a cash offer for it. I'm part of a local investment group that is buying houses, and yours would be a great fit for our portfolio.

- We purchase quickly.

- No fees or Realtor commissions.

- We purchase as-is (meaning you don't have to make any repairs).

- No appraisal contingency.

- If you are still interested in selling your house and receiving a no obligation cash offer, please contact us at your convenience. We look forward to hearing from you.

These letters are short and sweet. Put your contact information at the bottom of the letter, hand sign it, and mail it with a business card. I like to have these envelopes hand addressed, they have a much higher rate of being opened as people think it is a personal letter from someone they know, not just more junk mail. We'll talk a little more about that when we get to mailers. Make sure you mail to the actual owner's address, which is not always the physical address of the property. Pick one day a week to have your Realtor send you this list. It can be zip-code specific or your entire market area. It's just going to cost you some stamps, paper, and your time.

Bandit Signs

If you are not familiar with bandit signs, you should get familiar with them. These are the yellow signs that you see when you are driving down the road that are stapled to telephone poles, staked into the ground, or taped to stop signs. They typically say:

We Pay CASH for Houses

As-is, any condition

Phone number

There are lots of variations to these signs, and you can make them using old pieces of cardboard or special order them online from numerous different companies. I will be the first one to admit that these signs defy logic. Why would someone think that the person who is putting up a sign on an old refrigerator box using two different colors of marker has the money to buy their house for cash? Why would people even call the phone numbers on these signs? It basically comes down to the right-now effect. People are driving around worrying about money, worrying about the city or the bank taking their house away, and they are looking for a sign. Yes, that is a pun, but it is still a truth. They are looking for a sign, so why shouldn't it be your sign? Your bright yellow sign with bold black marker saying you will pay them cash for their house?

I know wholesalers all over the country who use bandit signs as their primary means of finding both sellers and buyers. It works. But it is also illegal in many markets, and you can get fined, and fined heavily, for each sign you put up. I've heard of people getting fined $500 to $1,000 per sign! Many cities have ordinances against posting advertising, and especially posting on city-owned property. That is why there is the possibility of fines. Bandit signs basically fall into the same category as littering or graffiti: you are being a public nuisance. Now that isn't true in all market areas, and it is very important for you to understand what you can and can't do in your marketplace and how to protect yourself. Some cities allow advertising on weekends, others don't. Many wholesalers will not put their actual cell phone number on the sign, they use an internet phone number that gets directed to their cell phone. There are a lot of different internet phone number providers that can give you different phone numbers that are redirected to your cell phone. It is a great tool to have for tracking calls from your various forms of marketing. I have at least twenty-five different numbers all being routed to my main marketing line, with a different number for each marketing channel. Bandit signs have their own number, and you can even go as far as putting different numbers on different bandit signs to know what part of town you are getting the most calls from. The great thing about this kind of number is they provide anonymity, as you can just cancel them if you start getting annoying or angry phone calls from anyone. I highly suggest you not use your main number on bandit signs.

Earlier I mentioned bandit signs get both sellers and buyers. That's right, you can build your buyers list from bandit signs as well. As someone who has been in this game for a long time, I quickly learned that the people posting bandit signs are not usually the people who are actually buying the properties. They are getting them under contract and then wholesaling them. You will get flippers calling your bandit signs, asking if you have any properties for sale. Be ready for that, and add them to your buyers list. I typically just tell them to text over their full information (name, email, phone number, and area where they buy), and I will send them anything I have. Asking them to text the info is much easier than having them repeat it ten times as you try to hear it correctly and write it down on a napkin while at your daughter's volleyball game. Just make sure that the internet phone numbers you are getting have the capabilities to send and receive text messages, as some services do not have that.

It's also a good idea to track where you are putting your bandit signs. There are a few different apps you can use for this, or you can just use a simple city map and thumb tacks and keep costs down. Either way, it's good to know where your signs are in case you ever want to (or are forced to) move them.

If you are going to be placing bandit signs, here are a few tips:

- Make your print bold enough to be read from across the street.

- Include your phone number (yes, I have seen signs where people forget to put any contact information. What a waste of time, energy, and money).

- If you place your signs up higher on telephone poles, they will stay up longer and not be removed by the city or homeless people as easily. Search online for long reach stapler or bandit sign stapler, and you will find YouTube videos or pictures and designs of what other people use. I've seen people with six-foot staplers.

- Try minor variations to your signs and see what works. This is called split testing. When you only change one thing, you learn what works better. Try using all of the words the same, but on both a yellow and white backing. If more calls come from the white bandit signs, you know that you should do more white signs for your next order. If you are spending marketing dollars, you want to make sure you are tracking everything. Don't make too many changes at one time, as that way you won't know what the better trigger was. I recommend only changing one thing at a time.

- Busy corners get more eyes, and put the signs so they can be seen by the flow of traffic.

- Be respectful of other people's signs, don't remove them or cover them up. There are enough properties out there for everyone.

With modern technology, you are going to start seeing even more digital bandit signs. These are typically movable billboards about the size of a big screen television, and they have a rotating ad display. You might find these at gas stations, sporting events, mall parking lots. There will be a small fee for these depending on the amount of exposure and the location of the sign, but it typically equates to the same as the cost of placing your own signs around town. The nice thing about the digital bandit signs is you don't have to worry about the legal placement of the sign as it is the advertising company that makes sure they are placed in proper locations.

Bird Dogs

You may have heard this term before. A bird dog is someone who is out in the neighborhoods finding properties for you. They generate leads for you. This could be all manner of people, from mail carriers to garbage men to your construction team (if you also flip) to your high school buddies looking to make a little extra money. They will typically send you an address and say this house looks vacant, damaged, or has a FSBO sign in the front yard, here is the address. Additionally, I request that people text me a picture of the house along with the address, that way I can put it into my marketing right away and don't have to drive anywhere myself. Sometimes you will get a lead from someone and it's not just the address, but it's the whole background on the house and the owner and it comes with a phone number. Those leads are awesome, it's basically someone giving you a deal on a silver platter. But do people do this for free? No, they expect payment for their work. It costs time and gas money to find houses. I know different people pay people differently for their leads. Some people pay a low amount for each lead that comes over, maybe a dollar per lead. You do have to manage your bird dogs heavily on these, as you don't want someone to just drive up and down a street and take pictures of every single house and then expect you to pay them $1,000 for a thousand bad leads. Tell them what you are looking for (I actually give mine examples in pictures and a list of items to look for), and if after the first fifty they aren't giving you good leads, pay them the $50 and tell them, "Thanks, but I don't need you anymore."

Other people pay their bird dogs only if the deal closes, usually in the $500 to $5,000 range, depending on how much of the deal was actually given to you, meaning just an address or the silver platter. You have to be careful with this scenario about how you do it, as in many areas this is considered paying someone a commission for performing real estate services. If they are getting paid a commission and are not licensed, you can possibly both be fined by your state's real estate authority. I pay my bird dogs for lead generation.

What bird dogs really comes down to is just letting more people know what you do and that you pay referral fees. The more people who know, the more ears and eyes will be open and the more leads that will come to you.

There are a lot of ways to find leads, and with little to no money. In this chapter, we talked about posting on social media, driving for dollars, door knocking, door hangars, FSBOs, expired listings, bandit signs, and bird dogs. We use all of these in our real estate business because they work. They can work individually or even better as a combination. The main thing these all have in common, besides being low cost, is that they focus on getting you out there, getting your name out there and getting your company out there. If people don't know you exist, how can they sell you a house?

CASH MORE CHECKS

- Social media should be done with purpose. What's your hook?

- Every no is one step closer to a yes.

- Leave some wiggle room in your offers.

- Keep your eyes (and ears) open, there is opportunity everywhere.

- Find a way to connect with sellers.

- The more people who know what you do, the more you can do!

- Know your market, know your laws, and know the game.

- Spend your time wisely!

CHAPTER 4

Build Your Lead-Generating Machine—
Scrooge McDuck Style

In the prior chapter, we discussed a lot of different ways to build leads for little to no money. You may just be starting out in this business and don't have the funds to put toward expensive marketing. The $20 to print business cards, plus the $100 to buy the materials for bandit signs determines what you get to eat for the next two weeks. There is no shame in that. There really is only shame in not trying to do more for you, for your family, and for your future. Do you spend an extra three hours watching football on the couch or do you go out Saturday morning and knock on some doors? What's the worst that could happen? You get some exercise and a few people yell at you? If you are already on social media, why not do it in a way that can improve your life? Stop liking other people's pictures of fancy cars and amazing vacations and start earning the money to do those things yourself! There are leads out there, and it's better to learn and perfect your craft on the free leads than on the ones you might be spending thousands of dollars for. And that brings us to Scrooge McDuck.

If you don't know who Scrooge McDuck is, he is a cartoon character based on Ebenezer Scrooge. If you don't know who Ebenezer Scrooge is, he is the character Scrooge McDuck is based on. See what I did there? That's called circular reasoning. It's a great way to end an argument or move on to a different topic. That may come in handy one day during a seller negotiation.

Back to Scrooge McDuck. Scrooge McDuck started off as shining shoes and built his own massive fortune, one that he could literally swim in. He could dive into his pile of gold coins and do the backstroke, but no matter how much money he had, he was still extremely frugal. That takes us into the lead channels that can cost money, a lot of money. If you aren't watching your money, what you spend on marketing, pretty soon your pile of gold coins could end up being back to that original nickel at the bottom of the pond. The basic premise here is if you are spending money, it had better be making you more money. That means that if you spend $1,000 on marketing and it brings in $1,000 or less in revenue, you have lost money.

When I am spending money on marketing, I like to see at a minimum a three-to-one return. That means that for every dollar I spend, I get at least three back. If I spend $1,000 I get $3,000 back, which becomes a $2,000 profit ($3,000 in revenue – $1,000 in cost = $2,000 in profit). At scale, if I can spend $10,000 in marketing I should be able to make $30,000 in revenue for a $20,000 profit! Now for some of you, that may not be enough, but remember, I said a minimum. My average is closer to a six-to-one return, meaning that for every $10,000 I spend, I profit $50,000 ($60,000 in revenue – $10,000 in cost = $50,000 in profit). We'll talk more about the math and tracking in a later chapter, but just know that if you aren't tracking your money, you are wasting money.

Throughout this chapter, I am going to talk a lot about different tech and ways to do things, but I am not going to give a lot of company names or providers, as they change so rapidly. Tech, if anything, is consistently changing. New apps are being created, and there are always new ways to do things, but the basic premise, the concept, is what I want you to understand. Once you understand it, it is as simple as posting on social media, on Facebook or Instagram (or whatever the next big thing is): "RVM? Who are you using and at what price?" or "Looking for a new skip trace service, who do you recommend?"

Typically, you will get a few solid answers from people who actually use the service and are happy to share. Post in several groups to get a variety of answers, and then interview the companies and compare them to your needs and budget. "*The Flipping Blueprint* Group" on Facebook is a good group to post in. Remember, these marketing tactics are the ones that are going to start eating up your marketing budget, but you have to be like Scrooge McDuck: frugal, but smart. Just because a company is the cheapest, doesn't mean they are the best. Once you interview the company, post on social media "What do you think of XYZ Skip Trace?" When people respond, don't just take their answer at face value, ask them direct follow-up questions about how they used the service, what the results were, and if they are still using them. These direct questions typically get a higher rate of answer if done through private messages.

Scrooge McDuck didn't want to spend his money, but when he did, he spent it on the best things.

Let's dig into some of these more expensive ways to make money. I recommend doing these one at a time, finding what works for you, and doubling down on that.

Cold Calling

If you have never cold called someone to sell them something, you have to try it. Think of all the telemarketer calls you have received from companies trying to sell you magazine subscriptions, offering credit cards, or letting you know you possibly won a Disney Cruise. How did you react to them? Were you always the most pleasant person? Did you yell at them? Did you hang up on them? I know I haven't always been the kindest to people making sales calls. Telemarketers call when you are at work, at dinner, or in the bathroom. Now if I have time, I will actually listen to the pitch and give them a minute to hook me, bring me in, and make their offer (I still won't buy, but you can always learn new things). If you have never seen the movie *Boiler Room* with Giovanni Ribisi, watch it and pay attention to the telemarketing call scene. You'll understand what I am talking about.

So how does cold calling actually work? Do you just open up the phone book and start at the beginning with Aaron Aaronson, call him up and say, "Hi my name is Luke and I want to know if you would like a cash offer for your house." Thanks to our tech friendly world, you do not have to do this. Let's start from the beginning. Who should you call? The best way to do this is to buy lists (only buy lists after hitting the free FSBOs mentioned in the previous chapter). Lists will vary in price, depending on what comes with them and how accurate they are as well as how many numbers you buy (quantity usually gets you a better price) and how in depth you go with the data. Some of the most popular lists to buy are:

- Notice of Default (NOD). These are people who are behind on their mortgage and have been sent a warning that the bank is getting ready to take their house away.

- Notice of Sale (NOS). These are people who are behind on their mortgage and the banks have scheduled a sale date to take their house away, usually within the next three or four weeks and typically at an auction. This is typically an extremely motivated seller group and you will have to act fast, as the clock is ticking.

- Probate or Inheritance. These are people who have inherited a property when a family member who was the owner of real estate has died.

- 60/10/2000. Homeowners who are sixty years or older, have owned a house for at least ten years, and the house is more than two-thousand square feet of living area. Basically, this list is looking for people who may be ready to downsize now that the kids have moved out. You can even throw "two--story" into the search, because as people get older, they typically like stairs less.

- Equity. This is a list that a lot of people get, but I have found issues with it, as it typically is not the most accurate, because it makes assumptions on remaining mortgage balance owed as well as using inaccurate indicators of present value. Basically, this list is supposed to be people who have money tied up in their house, perhaps the house is estimated to be worth $300,000 and records indicate the seller had a $220,000 mortgage taken out fifteen years ago. That mortgage theoretically has been paid down to approximately $170,000 so there is $130,000 of potential equity in the property ($300,000 − $170,000 = $130,000). What's wrong with this? Most of the time, the figure they are using for value is wrong, the total owed is just a guess, and may not include things like second mortgages, credit card debt, and so on.

- Free and Clear. This is for properties that have no recorded loans against them. These people typically have a lot of cash tied up in their properties, and selling is a good way to get it out. Additionally, a lot of people who own one property free and clear may own other properties. Add in "absentee" to make this an even better list.

- Vacant. Vacant homes are typically just costing people money. This is a great lead source, whether you are paying for a list or just driving for dollars. I buy and wholesale a lot of vacant houses.

- Delinquent Taxes. Similar to the NOD or NOS, these owners have not been paying their local real estate taxes and the city or county may be getting ready to take their house away.

These are just some of the lists that you can get. Typically, they aren't labeled as such and you will need to make various selections to create these lists, depending on what provider you are getting them from. Getting the list is just the first step, and really the first step of spending money. Different lists will cost different amounts. The more detailed you are, the more precise you are, the greater the cost (and usually the smaller number of names on the list). When we are talking lists, we aren't talking fifty or one hundred names, we are talking thousands, thousands of names—either local or national depending on what you are doing. Let's use the example of a list of ten thousand names. Do you typically get a list and then start calling people? No. Most of the lists do not have the most accurate data for phone numbers or emails. Many lists don't even come with those, they are just a list of addresses. Once you get a list, you will have to skip trace it. You have to hire a service to go through that list and look through online records and get you phone numbers and emails. With a starting list of ten thousand names, this amount could drop down to between two and eight thousand addresses total. I'll also scrub from my list, meaning remove, companies, banks, and LLCs that are the listed property owners, as well as making sure properties haven't been transferred in the past twelve months. This is especially important when talking about sending mailers. Do you want to send an extra two thousand mailers to addresses that you know aren't even interested in selling? Remember, you have to be smart and frugal with your money, not just use a shotgun approach. Additionally, many people will scrub their lists against the National Do Not Call Registry. These are people who have signed up to not be called by telemarketers. If you don't do this, you run the risk of fines from the government, which is just another thing to be aware of.

Now you have a list that you paid to purchase, and you paid another company to skip trace and scrub it, and the original ten thousand names you started with is down to six thousand names, addresses, and phone numbers, and may include basic property information such as size, room count, year purchased, purchase amount, and so on. Do you pick up the phone and start calling? You could, but how long before you get tired of dialing numbers? And what number are you even going to call them from? Your personal cell phone number? Not recommended. Yes, you can and probably will do this with a pad of paper, a phone, and a lot of drive when you are first starting, but when you are ready, you can build a call center.

Here is the basic set up of a call center. After you have input your list into your CRM (Customer Relationship Management program, this is the program you use to track everything), you have a phone service that has multiple phone lines for your company. It's all digital, and every phone call made is tracked for time and typically can even be recorded. You have a computer dialing system that is constantly dialing phone numbers for you (no pesky punching in the buttons on your phone for your callers). Your callers (two to eight people, depending on your scale and budget) are sitting at their computer screens with headsets on. Your computer dials the numbers (and it can dial several numbers at a time). When a call is picked up, it hangs up any other out-bound calls, and your caller looks at their computer screen and the property information is showing on the CRM they are using and the conversation begins.

A lot of people at this point will have their callers use an opening line, not really a script. The opening line can be "I'm part of a real estate-investing firm buying properties in your area and we saw that you are the owner of a property at 123 Any Street, is that accurate? Would you be interested in a cash offer for your property?" Or the more direct approach, "Is this Mike? Do you own the property at 123 Any Street? Would you be interested in a cash offer for it?" There really are several different ways to start your opening line, but from my experience it really is personality based. What works for one salesperson doesn't always work for the one sitting right next to him. Cold callers typically have to go through several hundred phone calls before they start to feel comfortable and know that their opening line works for them. This will be a trial and error process, so just be prepared for it. Once your caller has them on the hook, that's when they get into the questionnaire. Again, this really isn't a script, it's a list of questions to help you determine their motivation to sell and how hot the lead is. In our office, we rank leads on a three-level list: cold, warm, or hot. Why is this important? Because time is important. You don't want to waste a lot of time on cold leads, which could be someone who still lives in their house, is currently listed with a Realtor, and is not looking to move any time soon. A warm lead would be someone who has a vacant house, they are in between renters, and are deciding if they want to rent it again or fix it up and sell it. A hot lead is someone who just got a notice of foreclosure, the bank is telling them they are going to take the house from them in forty-five to ninety days, and are afraid they are going to lose everything and not receive any money. In my office, we schedule every warm and hot lead for a property inspection.

Here is a list of questions we ask when we have someone on the phone:

- Confirm the address.

- Confirm actual ownership (you want to make sure you are talking with the decision maker, the person who actually owns the house, or at least one of the people on the title).

- Confirm the basic features of the house. (I see your house has four bedrooms and two bathrooms and is 1,620 square feet. Is that correct?).

- Confirm the condition of the house. (How is everything working in the house? Have you repaired or replaced anything lately?).

- Confirm that the house is not listed with a Realtor. (Is your house currently listed with a Realtor? Have you listed your house in the past two years?).

- Ask what they think their house is worth ("Do you have any idea on what your house is worth?"). If they think their house is worth a hundred and fifty thousand dollars and your records indicate two hundred and fifty thousand dollars, that is a hot lead!

- Talk about a time frame for them to move out. (If we were to make a cash offer today, how long would you need to move?) We offer our sellers the option of staying in the house for up to thirty days, free of cost, after the house is sold. This allows them to sell the house, get money in their pocket, and be able to move in their time frame.

- Set up an appointment for an inspector to visit the house. (Are you available to show one of our inspectors the property today/tomorrow?) This is only for warm or hot leads. If you know who the inspector is actually going to be, I prefer to share that name immediately, that way it is more personable right from the start. *Gary?* the homeowner thinks. *Great, I can't wait to meet Gary and get his cash offer!* That is better than having the homeowner think, *I wonder who is going to be coming out to my house tomorrow. I didn't even get their name.*

Your cold caller then puts the property on the schedule for your inspector to see the property. Again, this is all done within the CRM tracking program. This really is a brief rundown on cold calling, which in itself could be its very own book. There are many different ways to set up call centers, either in person or virtual (yes, you can have Virtual Assistants living overseas doing these initial phone calls and even making offers for you!). But as you can see, there is a cost associated with every step along the way. You are paying for a list, you are paying for skip tracing, you are paying for a CRM, you are paying for a call system, you are paying for phone numbers, you are paying for a dialing system, you are paying for a virtual calling system, you are paying your callers, you are paying your call manager, you are paying your property inspector, you are paying a lot, and that is why volume is the key. Once you set up a call center, you need to keep feeding it more and more leads.

You can create a fully automated call center, or you can just dial the numbers yourself. Either way, cold calling works. You can reach more people in more areas, and you can really build a pipeline from cold calling. There is a reason why people do this, because when it is done well, it is profitable. A couple things to note, if you are doing a call center with virtual assistants, just remember that they are only as good as their training. Take the time to train them and make sure you record their calls so you can spot-check them.

If you are not getting results, a lot of times the problem starts with your list. You could have the best cold callers in the world, but if they don't have a good list to work with, you are just burning money. Get a good list, track the number of calls you are making and the number of bad phone numbers, track the number of conversations your people have, listen to their conversations, read their notes, and most importantly, make appointments and get in the door! Note: if you have a lot of bad phone numbers you have a bad skip-tracing company and may be entitled to a refund, but you won't get it unless you ask for it. What happens if the seller is not local to the property and neither are you? You can still make an offer, site unseen! Your cold caller schedules a phone appointment for you to call them back with the offer. You can even send the contract to them for digital signatures. Open your eyes to the possibilities of how you can do this business, and you will see entirely new revenue streams.

With cold calling, it is fine to make offers right on the phone. I know a lot of wholesalers who do this and get deals locked up. Now, if you are making an offer and having someone sign a contract without having someone see the property, just make sure that you have enough time built into your contract to have someone go out and view the property. Additionally, you will want to be able to back out or renegotiate your contract if you find the deal doesn't pencil out once you actually get eyes on the property. Typically in these scenarios, you are putting more properties under contract and closing fewer of them, as you will have to go back and renegotiate the deals during your due-diligence timeframe.

Mailers

I recently heard from a new wholesaler who had just left a big, fancy seminar that "Mailers are dead." If that is the case, why do I still get deals from mailers? I actually hear this same statement about every type of marketing or advertising that is out there, but they all work. They really do, you just have to put in the effort.

Mailers can be a great way to automate your marketing with very little work on the front end. You will still need to buy lists and scrub them like we mentioned before, but now you are going to send that list to a professional company that automates your entire mailing campaign. They will take your list of addresses, plan typically a five-to-seven-stage mailing program and send out various letters, postcards, and notices to each address either five or seven times. Why five or seven? Because statistically you have to be put in front of someone that many times for the chance of a sale to occur. If you are only mailing someone once, you are typically just throwing money away! Now this is where the Scrooge McDuck style of marketing comes in, because mailers can be expensive. If, on average, each piece of mail you send out is just $1 (that pays for the labor, paper, envelope, stamp, ink, lists, skip tracing, and so on) and you are mailing to a list of two thousand addresses, that is $2,000 just for the first batch. Now remember, we are going to send mailers out five to seven different times to the same list. Each batch will be sent somewhere between two and four weeks apart. That's $10,000 to $14,000 for one campaign spread out over three months or so. But that is just one campaign and, ideally, you have multiple campaigns running at any given time.

Mailers are definitely a numbers game. Small, unfiltered batches of addresses will not get you the results you want and will just eat up your marketing budget. The more successful wholesalers typically start their budgets in the $20,000 range, and I know wholesaling companies that spend well over $100,000 every month just on their direct mail campaigns. If direct mail is dead, why do they spend so much? Because they get results! They also mitigate their costs. They know that if you have returned mail, that needs to come off your mailing lists. If you have a list of two thousand addresses and between the first two batches you send out you get two hundred mailers returned as undeliverable, you had better remove those from your next mailing batches. Let's do the math on that. If you are scheduled to mail each address seven time for a campaign, and between batch two and batch three you have accumulated two hundred returned letters, there are still five mailing batches to go. At $1 per piece of mail, that equals $2,000 (200 x 5 x $1 = $2,000). You will save by taking the time to remove those from your address list.

So, what do you do with those returned mailers? Toss them in the garbage? Most wholesalers do. And guess what? A lot of wholesalers mail to the same addresses that you will mail to. Most everyone is buying the same, or similar, lists. If you are mailing a Notice of Default (NOD) list, chances are that same address is getting mailers from more than ten other wholesalers or flippers, too! This is why I don't just throw out our returned mail. Since almost everyone else is doing that, we actually skip trace what is returned to us. When we do that, we are now mailing to a new address for that potential owner (or cold calling them) and more than likely we have reduced our competition to next to nothing as seven or eight of the other ten people mailing this person are not doing this. Now it's just between me and one or two other people. Return mail can be gold, but at the very least, make sure you remove it from your lists so you don't just throw away money mailing to the same address that keeps sending them back as undeliverable. Remember, smart but frugal!

Don't over think your mailing campaigns, either. I know wholesalers who swear by the different mailer approach and have a mix of the postcards, handwritten envelopes, warning letters, past due letters, and so on in their campaigns, and I know others who use the exact same mailer for all five or seven hits. Both are very successful. You can keep it simple or make it complicated, but one question to always ask the people who call you is, "Where did you get our number?" You want, and you need, to know what pieces of your marketing are working best for you. If it works, repeat, repeat, repeat!

Ringless Voice Mails (RVM) and Short Message Services (SMS)

Over the last few years, these two forms of marketing have become increasingly popular, so what are they? Have you ever looked at your phone and saw that you had a voicemail, but you never heard your phone ring or saw a missed call? Maybe it came in while you were on another call or maybe when you were driving through a dead spot. You check the voicemail and it is someone you don't know trying to sell you something or offer you free tickets to Disney or someone saying they are the IRS and they need to meet you at 7-Eleven with a cashiers check to pay off unpaid taxes, otherwise the police will be coming to your door? These are ringless voice mails (RVM). You can hire a service to deliver a message to tens of thousands of phone numbers at a time. It saves you time from having the same conversation over and over with multiple people. Now you can just deliver a voicemail, and if they are interested, they can call you back! This allows you to reach thousands of people with your message in the time it would have taken you to dial ten phone numbers and maybe have one conversation. You can leave a simple message along the lines of "Good morning, this is Sally. I wanted to talk to you in further detail about the cash offer on your house. Call me back at 123-456-7890." Or you can leave a two-to-three-minute message that goes in depth on the service you are offering, the process, how it benefits them, and how you are different from the rest. The thought process between the short message or long message is that a short message is just a teaser and will get more people calling back, but, the long message will typically get a more motivated, more serious group calling back. Both work, and really will depend on who is answering the phone when these people call back. But just like door knocking, mailers, or any other sort of advertising, be prepared for people to call back and be upset! One additional step you can take in this, especially when they call back after the short teaser message, you can have that go to an answering machine that has the more in-depth process explained there and then, if they are really interested in selling their home, they have a chance to either leave a message or press one to be connected with a live acquisitions manager. Most people won't stay on the phone for three minutes just to tell you to get bent. They will stay on the phone because they need to sell their property.

Short Message Service (SMS), better known as texting, is a marketing method where you can send mass text messages out, again to tens of thousands of numbers at a time, with a teaser message. Some messages I have seen can be as simple as "Hey, are you having a good day?" or "Did you have time to talk about the cash offer on your house?" Others can be more detailed, such as "My name is John and I want to give you a cash offer on your home. No obligation and it takes about five minutes, respond yes if you would like to schedule a time to discuss." The beauty of RVM and SMS is that when compared to a mailer at $1 per piece, you can do these for pennies or even less than a penny each. But there is a lot of additional tracking, servicing, and peripheral expenses that can add up with these. Additionally, you aren't hitting a list of two thousand numbers when you are doing these, you are hitting lists of ten, fifty, or one hundred thousand numbers at a time! This really is a shotgun approach. But be cautious, with any new innovation comes new regulation. If you are sending to the wrong people, especially those on the Do Not Call list, you could incur fines. It's best to know how to do this right and understand the risks before you get into it. Interview multiple companies before choosing one.

Social Media Ads

Facebook and Instagram are the main social media platforms I see other wholesalers spending time and money on. Most of them have very little success, as they think they can just pay $100 and run an ad themselves and they will get the calls or clicks. That is not the way this works. Successful social media marketing is based on extensive and complicated algorithms and demographic data to make sure your content is getting in front of the correct audience. I highly suggest that if you are going to do this, find a company that specializes in running these campaigns for you, as this is a specialty skill set. When interviewing companies, make sure they have run campaigns for other wholesalers or flippers before, that way they understand your target audience, how to find them, and how to get in front of them with something they want to click on. This can be a very expensive process and can take time. Have you ever done an internet search for a pair of shoes? A car? A restaurant? You may have searched once on your computer or your phone, but then you start seeing the item you searched for everywhere you go. You see it on your Facebook account, you see it on Google when you are looking up something completely different, and you see it as an ad on your Instagram. It is everywhere. That's because the original ad you clicked on was set up correctly, and now that advertiser is retargeting you and your accounts so that you will see it everywhere. Click on that link, and it may even take you to a different website than the one you were on before, but for the same company. It might even say "Welcome Back," because it knows you were there before. That is how we have our ads running. If you clicked once, when you click on our retargeting campaign it takes you to a different web page to further entice you to finally fill out our form if you didn't do it before. Your social media ads should grab attention and funnel people to your websites, and your websites should entice people to fill out forms with their contact information. If this doesn't sound complicated at all, try doing it yourself. If it does sound complicated, hire a professional. That is what we do, and it is worth the money when you find the right person.

Pay Per Click (PPC)

Pay Per Click (PPC) is online advertising. It's the ads you see when you are browsing the web or it is the top searches you see when you are using a search engine. You can advertise on all of the different search engines, Google, Bing, Yahoo, and so on. There are services that can run your campaigns for you and, depending on your marketing budget, they typically charge between $500 and $5,000 a month. I personally love PPC. The reason why is because you typically get fewer angry people yelling at you for interrupting their dinner and more people who are truly interested in selling their homes. They have to reach out to you. You are not reaching out to them, but with PPC you are just letting them know you are there if they are looking for you. A typical setup will have some sort of lead generation or funnel that brings the leads into your CRM, and then you reach out to the lead and try to close the deal. We use multiple lead generators, some as simple as asking people for their name and phone number so we can call them back and others that are more in-depth with multiple questions about their home, why they want to sell, what they think it's worth, and so on. Again, just like mailers, RVM, or cold calling, there are services out there that can help and automate all of this for you, it really just depends on how much you want to spend.

One of the main differences with PPC (and social media ads) versus the other marketing methods is the way you target your audience. When you are cold calling or mailing, you are doing it from a targeted list, you aren't just picking up a phone book (do they still have those?). With PPC, you want to go after a targeted audience, a demographic, a specific region, or based on specific key words that someone types when doing a web search. Some of the key words we go after are phrases like "sell my house fast," "sell my Vegas home," "cheap listing service," and so on. There are many, many different phrases and keywords, but if people aren't contacting you, if they aren't clicking on your link, you are not getting in front of the right people. We actually review and revise our campaigns weekly to make sure we are making the most of our PPC budget. Spend, but spend wisely!

Once those leads come in, you do have to reach out to them immediately, because what does the internet give people? Choices! If they contacted you, most likely they contacted three to five other buyers or wholesalers as well. Get on the phone and start your process as fast as you can. We typically do a quick, preliminary search on the property they submitted if an address came with their form, determine an ARV, and then determine a maximum purchase price. Depending on how the conversation goes, we may make an offer on the phone or we may schedule an immediate time to see their property. You most likely will have competition and other people calling this lead, so be quick and be prepared. The seller will be more apt to go with the person who is nicest and most knowledgeable.

Remember, the goal is to help them solve their problem, the solution is getting their house under contract so you can wholesale it!

I can tell you for a fact that I am not an expert in any of the lead engines I just described, but the cool thing is, I don't have to be. I spend my time being an expert in real estate, and then I hire experts in various fields to do what they do best. I care very little overall for tech, although tech is a huge part of my business now. From social media platforms to automated mailings to keyword analytics to market demographics, it all matters. You should still know how to understand your numbers, your Key Performance Indicators (KPI), but a good expert who you hire is going to tell you where your numbers are and how they compare within your industry.

Don't hire someone who has only done marketing for a sports beverage company to do the marketing for your real estate-investing company. Find someone experienced in your field! Again, the best way to do that is to ask. Ask on social media, Twitter, Facebook, Instagram, and so on. Ask multiple times, and you will find the right people who can manage your marketing campaigns. There is almost nothing worse than spending tens of thousands of dollars on marketing and getting zero results. Many of us have done that over the years, and that has helped perfect a lot of the marketing available to you today. You get the benefits of past investors' mistakes. That is why finding an experienced marketer is great. I prefer marketing companies that are smaller and have a few successful clients in multiple markets, that way you get a more hands-on approach as they still feel every client matters. If you go to some of the bigger marketing companies, you will just be another call on their daily log. If you don't feel like they are taking care of you and aren't making time for you, they are not the right fit. Remember, when you hire an expert, you are the client. They are not doing you a favor, you are paying them for a service, so make sure you get what you are paying for.

CASH MORE CHECKS

- Spend your money wisely.

- Know your returns. Making $700 from spending $1,000 is losing $300!

- Ask for help and then follow up!

- Everything works as long as you work.

- If you are going to train someone, make sure you know how to do it yourself first.

- You don't have to be the expert, but do hire an expert.

CHAPTER 5

You Have Leads, How Do You Know
if You Have a Real Deal?

Once you start letting people know what you do, the leads will start coming in. So how do you know if it's is a real deal? A seller calls you, or returns your phone call, you get through the initial pleasantries, and when you ask them "How much do you want for your house?" they tell you $80,000. Now what? Is this a good deal? The real answer is yes, it is a good deal, because you at least have a number to start working with. So lets dig into it, because every property has different exit strategies. We touched on this a little bit earlier in the book, some of the exit strategies are, you could sell to:

- A fix and flipper

- A private landlord looking for rentals

- A hedge fund building a portfolio (these are the groups from Wall Street with a bazillion dollars)

- Joe and Jane Homebuyer

There are actually more options than these, but these are the top four that you will look to, as they are the most standard and easiest to deal with. Knowing that you have multiple options can really help, although each property will have a best-suited buyer. So, let's look at that list again and see what properties are best suited for which buyer.

A Fix and Flipper. These investors are open to all level of damage, from a little carpet and paint to repairing burned-out properties. Each flipper has their own different comfort levels, but they will be the ones typically buying if there is more than just a lipstick remodel needed on a property.

A Private Landlord. Most small landlords, people with fewer than twenty rental properties in their portfolio, tend to invest in what they know. If they have other rentals in that same neighborhood, they are a potential buyer for your property. They will be more selective on what they buy, and typically don't want more than a lipstick remodel. Many times, they are just looking for property that is rent-ready. Although a landlord will typically pay more than a fix and flipper, they are most likely going to be pickier on what they buy.

A Hedge Fund. Hedge funds have their own specific formulas for the rental properties they purchase. Depending on their buying cycle they are in, they may be buying everything or they may have already established themselves in a marketplace and know the specific areas where they get the best rent and return, planned future appreciation, and will be more set in their ways. Over the last few years, I have seen a shift with my hedge fund buyers and have found them buying more of the lipstick-only properties versus full remodels. They have realized they make less money when managing large rehabs, and most just aren't good at it.

Joe and Jane Homebuyer. This is the most specific buyer type and, in most cases, you will already have a relationship with them prior to having the house. This way you know what they are looking for specifically and you can go out and find properties that most closely match their criteria. Some people call this reverse wholesaling, as you find the buyer first and then you narrow your focus to the product they want.

Now you know there are different buyers and they are looking for different things. Great, but you still don't know if $80,000 is a good deal for this house. First, you need to find out what the market value is, or in the investing language, the After Repair Value (ARV). There are a few quick ways to do this (I do go into much more depth in *The Flipping Blueprint* on this, as it pertains to house flippers), so let's run down the basics. But before I do that, just know that most of the automated sites that give a value for a house, such as Zillow, Redfin, iComps, and even most of the CRMs that have a valuation tool, are wrong. It's just the way it is as they are using mass data versus the most similar properties available. They use averages when specifics are the more accurate way to determine a value of a property. However, and I cringe when I type this, they can still give you a reasonable starting point and can be a quick and valuable tool in your tool belt, as long as you know how to use them. Additionally, they are also faster than waiting for a Realtor to get you a value determination. You have the address and you know the seller wants $80,000. They explained the house is in decent shape and just needs a little updating. Here are some free sites you can visit to get some baselines for value. You basically just have to type the address into the form and it will show you an estimated value.

- www.zillow.com

- www.redfin.com

- www.realestateabc.com

- www.iComps.com

Of these, I prefer iComps and Zillow as I can look at the comparable sales they are showing me and easily weed out the ones that are not similar and then narrow it down to the most similar closed sales and most recent sales to determine my ARV. The original estimate might have been $142,769, but that included five newer properties and four with pools. Once I remove those, I get a truer value of $130,000, based on three recently closed sales of similar age, living area, design, and features (think apple-to-apple comparison). Remember, this is the After Repair Value, meaning what the house will be worth after it is fixed up, so when looking for comparable sales you want to find ones that are in good shape, not run down. Recent remodels and flips would be ideal indicators to base your ARV on.

So why do you need to know the ARV? That way you can determine how much you can make. The ARV is the starting point of the equation, and you subtract everything from that. In this case, if your ARV is $130,000 and the seller is asking for $80,000, that leaves $50,000 on the table. Where does that $50,000 go? It really depends on your end buyer and the condition of the property. Let's break this down to some usable numbers, and if you read *The Flipping Blueprint* you will notice this is a very different tactic on wholesale deals than it is when you are calculating your own flip numbers. Why is that? Because you have a different goal. In this case, you are trying to make the largest assignment fee while still giving value to your end buyer. If there is no value, why would they buy it? It has to be a win-win scenario.

Let's break it down:

ARV

- 10 percent of ARV for closing costs and transaction fees

- Repairs

- 10 percent of ARV for profit

- Purchase price

= Your assignment fee

Now this equation may be a little different than some of the ones you see out there that are trying to derive the max offer you can produce. Some of those formulas might be similar to:

ARV x 70 percent – Repairs = Max allowable
offer – Desired assignment fee

OR

ARV x 65 percent – Repairs = Offer price

They all vary, and they can all be accurate and get you where you want to go as long as you understand them. My personal way of looking at it is based on this thought, *How big of an assignment fee can I make?* That's why, at the end of my equation the answer is, "Your Assignment Fee." It's just a different way to look at it, but most of the time you will have a potential purchase price established before you can start calculating your fee. Do you count your chickens before they hatch?

How should you calculate repairs? Do you have to be an expert in construction? No. Keep it simple. The best way is to lump properties into four categories and use a price-per-foot method to determine a repair estimate. You do have to realize that every buyer will do something different to a property and will have a different goal or end game and what they do to the property will also affect the final ARV or final sale price for the property. One flipper may just do a lipstick remodel for $8,000, while another does a full remodel at the cost of $40,000. The house will have different sale prices depending on what is done to it. Also, some flippers may overpay for their remodels and spend $70,000 when they could have done it for $40,000. All of that is beyond your control. Your job in estimating repairs as the wholesaler is to just give a reasonable idea of the condition and calculate that into a working number to see if it is a deal.

This is how you keep it simple. Put every house you see into one of four categories and adjust as shown.

- **Good.** House is in good shape, lived in and clean. Plan for $5 per square foot of living space in repairs. This will cover paint, carpet, and a few minor issues. If you have a fifteen hundred square foot house, you would have a repair estimate of $7,500.

- **Fair.** House is a bit outdated and needs to be updated and remodeled. Items are broken, but not destroyed. It is being lived in, but you wouldn't want to live there. Plan for $10 per square foot of living space in repairs.

If you have a fifteen hundred square foot house, you would have a repair estimate of $15,000.

- **Bad.** It smells and you have to hold your breath, everything needs to be replaced. No one should be living here, but sometimes they still are. Plan for $15 per square foot of living space in repairs. If you have a fifteen hundred square foot house, you would have a repair estimate of $22,500.

- **Ugly.** No one can live here, it needs a full remodel and mechanicals have been stripped, windows broken, and you can smell the gross through the pictures. Plan for $20 per square foot of living space in repairs. If you have a fifteen hundred square foot house, you would have a repair estimate of $30,000.

Could someone come into that same Ugly house and say it needs $60,000 in repairs and remodeling? Yes. Could someone come in and use basic material, maybe some used equipment from storage, and just make it livable and rentable for $20,000? Probably. Will calling the house ugly and needing a full remodel with an estimate of $30,000 in repairs give your potential buyer enough to consider this property? Definitely.

All right, so let's put our formula to work on this deal.

$150,000 (ARV)

- $15,000 (10 percent of ARV for consideration of purchase and sale closing costs)

- $15,000 (Fair condition house, $10 per foot for 1,500 square feet)

- $15,000 (10 percent of ARV for buyer's profit)

- $80,000 (purchase price)

= $25,000 assignment fee potential

So, what do you try to sell this deal at? That would be the purchase price plus your assignment fee. In this case, that would be $80,000 + $25,000 for $105,000. You may have buyers take it at $105,000, or you might get offers at $90,000. You have to decide how much you want to make. Sometimes you sell your deals and make $0 or maybe only $500, probably not even enough to cover your marketing costs and your time. But sometimes you have to take those deals to move on to the next one. Other times you may hit a home run and get a $100,000 assignment fee.

Now, if you inspect the property and find out this property is in ugly condition, and you estimated repairs at $30,000, you can always offer less on the purchase price. Instead of $80,000, offer them $70,000. What you get the property under contract for is really the variable that will determine how much you make for an assignment fee. The better you negotiate the purchase price, the bigger the assignment fee you can charge.

Now, I can speak from years of experience from being on both sides of wholesale transactions that when you supply any type of number, whether it is your ARV, repair estimate, rent estimate, or any estimate at all, your potential buyers will question it. Don't be offended by that, you should expect it! They need to make sure they are getting a deal that works for them, too. That's why I like to give less information, as I know the real buyers who are out there are capable of doing their own research. I still get deals from other wholesalers that have five pages of documentation on how they came up with their numbers, why they think they are accurate, and why I should believe them. I don't even look at these, as I know they are garbage. Real buyers do their own research. You have to put enough information in your presentation to pass their initial smell test. If it passes, they will do their research and contact you.

One thing that standard formulas don't show is the different results each property can have. I can tell you that there are a lot of rental buyers out there who have paid more for properties than I would have. When you are marketing to your buyers, it's good to know what your buyer's end results are. The repairs a flipper will do to a property are much different than those a landlord will do, still different than those that an AirBnB buyer will do, and even more different than those that a retail homeowner will do. Additionally, it is always easier to drop your price than it is to raise it. If you are asking someone to pay $180,000, don't go back to them and ask if they can now pay $185,000. Start at $190,000 and see what offers come in.

One of the main things you have to remember is if the seller wants to sell, lock it up. If they are ready to sign, get that contract signed, even if you think the price won't work out. That's right, if you have an ARV of $400,000, you made them an offer at $270,000 and they said they have to have $350,000 otherwise they aren't signing it, get it signed. Let them know what you are going to do though. I tell sellers, "Listen, for me to be the end buyer I would have to be at $270,000, but I have other partners in my network who buy rentals or who I partner with, and I think they are still going to be interested in this. Let's put it under contract at your $350,000 and I will present it to them. The reason why we need to put it under contract is because these are serious buyers, and they do not look at properties unless they are already under contract. I will put it in front of a few of my select partners and will let you know in a few days if we can continue to move forward. If not, we cancel the contract and you can try listing on the open market with a Realtor." Lock those contracts up and you'll be surprised, sometimes those properties you thought would never move at such a high price will sell immediately. That's because there are different buyers with different end strategies. Don't limit yourself.

CASH MORE CHECKS

- If a seller wants to sell, lock it up.

- Your negotiation on the purchase price determines your assignment fee.

- Your buyers have to profit, too.

- Keep your estimates reasonable, your buyers are smart.

- Don't be afraid to renegotiate a deal.

- Different buyer types have different purchasing criteria and calculate their profit based on their exit strategies. Get multiple buyers from each exit strategy and sell more deals.

- Keep your repairs simple, you never really know what your end buyer will do.

CHAPTER 6

What Kind of Closer Are You?

Are you tough or do you love? Are you going to make someone cry or cry with them? If these two sentences just freaked you out, don't worry. There is plenty of in-between on how to close deals. In a prior chapter, I talked briefly about one of my closing techniques, but you have to know that everyone has their own style of closing that works for them. Just like when we talked about opening lines for cold callers, what works for one person doesn't always work for the person next to them.

I was once told by someone who thought he was the best salesperson on earth that he could "close ninety percent of the people if they were ready to sign right then and there." It reminded me of the statement from the historical documentary *Anchorman* when a news anchor proclaims "sixty percent of the time it works every time." These statements have two things in common:

1. Both are nonsensical, and when you really look at them that is clear. If someone is ready to sign right

then and there, how come you can only close the sale ninety percent of the time? And if something only works sixty percent of the time, every time, doesn't that mean it doesn't work forty percent of the time?

2. If both of these statements are said with confidence, they aren't questioned!

No matter what type of closer you are, you have to have confidence, even if internally you are still questioning things. Maybe you still don't believe in yourself. Maybe you don't believe they will like you. Maybe you don't believe they will sign a contract. Maybe you don't believe you ran your numbers right. Maybe you don't believe you can sell the deal after they sign. Maybe, maybe, maybe! It's okay to question yourself, but don't let the seller know or sense it. Speak with confidence and soon enough, even when you stumble over your own words and accidentally say your own "sex panther" reference (that's the *Anchorman* quote above, did you actually believe I was quoting a real historical documentary?), it will make sense to the seller and they won't question it and will move on and put that pen to the paper. Be confident. The seller contacted you because you are the expert.

So how do you actually close? What is needed? First and foremost, the best way to make a sale is by not talking! That's right, shut up and let the seller sell. But if you are not talking you had better be listening. Find out what their emotional drive is. Why do they not only want to sell, but why do they have to sell?

Here are a few different sales techniques or styles, but remember, you will need to find your own voice.

- **The Novice.** If you are old enough to know the TV show *Columbo*, this is the perfect example. "Just one last question," was how this detective always solved the case. If you play the novice, you can still be an actual expert but you are turning the tables and basically making the seller feel sorry for you and selling to you because they are now the ones helping you out versus the other way around.

- **The Compassionate.** Do you cry when other people cry? This might be you. This isn't a style to fake, it has to be genuine, but it will help you close deals when people know that you truly do care about them and their position.

- **The Parent.** Some sellers need a mother or father figure to come in and tell them what is going to be best for them and guide them through the process. This has nothing to do with age. You could be twenty and the seller could be sixty, and you could still fit this role. The seller got themselves into some kind of trouble, and they need help from you.

- **The Forceful.** Do you like to tell people how it is? No bullshit, just straight to the point. Can you be definitive and direct and make people both understand and believe in you? This is the way.

- **The Confident.** Now, cocky is different than confident and cocky doesn't close deals. This is best done as a mix of the Compassionate and the Forceful. You know that this is the best choice for the seller and they believe you with all their heart and mind.

- **The Fear Monger.** Focus on the scary and bad that
  can happen if they don't sell to you. "They are going
  to take your house and kick you out on the street and
  then what? You are going to wish you had sold to me!"
  "This property is in such bad shape I'm surprised no
  one has died here yet!" This isn't my sales approach,
  but I know people who use it and close deals.

- **The Bob Ross** ("Let's paint a pretty picture"). Focus
  on their life after they sell to you. No more headaches
  from bad tenants. No more repairs. You'll get to move
  closer to your family which is your dream. You'll have
  plenty of money from the sale of the house to buy that
  golden alligator and ride it off into the sunset sur-
  rounded by happy trees!

There are lots of different techniques you can have in a sales
meeting or on a call, and it will take many of these meetings
and calls to find your voice and your closing method. The main
point you have to understand is that no matter what situation
the seller is in, their problems will be solved by signing a contract with you. It really is as simple as that.

Divorce? Sign this contract and move on with your separate
lives.

Bad tenants? Sign this contract and don't worry about
missed rent or bad toilets.

Death in the family? Sign this contract and don't worry
about this property and siblings fighting over the house. It's easier to split up money than a property.

Missed payments? Sign this contract and get your money out
of the house before the bank steals all of your equity in late fees.

Too much stuff? Sign this contract and leave it all behind. We'll donate it to charity and clean it up.

Lonely? Sign this contract and move closer to your friends, family, sports team, whatever.

Behind on taxes? Sign this contract and get a fresh start on your life with some money in your pocket.

Kid doing badly in school? Sign this contract and stop worrying about money so you can spend time with your kid and their homework versus stressing about bills.

Roof is missing one shingle? Sign this contract and don't worry about trying to hire a contractor who is going to steal from you and take advantage of you. We can handle all of the repairs once we have bought it.

It really doesn't matter what the problem is, the solution is signing the contract with you!

CASH MORE CHECKS

- Find your voice.

- Shut up and let the seller sell.

- Listen.

- Speak with confidence, you are the expert.

- Find the problem, and the solution is always for the seller to sell the house.

- You are a problem solver.

CHAPTER 7

Paperwork, Paperwork, Paperwork!

Why are so many people afraid of paperwork? It doesn't have to be scary, and it doesn't have to be complicated. Here are two different contracts that I use and have used in multiple states across the country. One is basic and simple and the other is more complicated and has more cover-your-ass terms in it. Pick the one that you understand and can close with.

Option #1 (Keep it Simple. One page, nice and easy)

REAL ESTATE CONTRACT OF SALE

THIS AGREEMENT OF SALE made this ___day of _____ 2020 by and between:_____ (Seller) and _____(Buyer)

WITNESS that the said Seller does hereby bargain and sell unto the said Buyer, and the Buyer does hereby agree to purchase the following property known as: 123 Any Street, Las Vegas, NV 89100

Seller agrees to sell the property for the price of $55,000 (Fifty-five thousand). $500.00 will be held as an Earnest Money Deposit (EMD) payable to the settlement company with the full balance due at closing. Buyer will be responsible for all standard closing costs, Seller will be responsible for any liens or past due accounts. Closing will take place on or before 30 business days from mutual execution of this contract. Closing date may be extended if title company is waiting on any encumbrances or liens to be cleared. This contract is fully assignable.

The property is sold in its "as is" condition and is subject to a 15-day inspection period starting from the notification of mutual execution of this contract. Seller will allow access to the property during this time period to allow Buyer to conduct inspections as they see fit.

TITLE. Title to the property shall be good and merchantable, free of liens and encumbrances and insurable.

POSSESSION. Possession of the premises shall be given to the Buyer at closing. If property is not vacated, Buyer reserves the right to extend the length of this contract until the time the property is vacated unless otherwise agreed herein. Buyer reserves the right to conduct a final inspection prior to closing.

RISK OF LOSS. The property is to be held at the risk of Seller until legal title has passed or possession has been given to the Buyer. If, prior to the time title has passed or possession has been given to Buyer, all or a substantial part of the property is destroyed or damaged, without the fault of the Buyer, then this contract, at the option of the Buyer shall be null and void and of no further effect, and all monies paid hereunder shall be returned promptly by Seller to the Buyer. If property is damaged, Buyer reserves the right to still purchase the property and negotiate with the Seller to reach a mutually agreed new purchase price. Buyer reserves the right to insure the property during the life of this contract to protect their interest.

Seller Signature _____Date_____

Seller Printed Name_____

Buyer Signature _____Date_____

Buyer Printed Name _____

In option 1, you have minimal fields to fill in, minimal items to explain, and it really is just one page of basic information. A property, a price, a timeframe, and a buyer and a seller. You'll find some sellers prefer to keep it simple, while others will look at this contract and not believe it can be so easy. Remember, the last time this person bought this house, they probably signed a hundred different documents.

For the savvier seller, you may want to go with option 2. It's longer and has more legal jargon, and basically looks more legitimate.

Option #2 (The CYA One)

Real Estate Purchase Agreement

This Real Estate Purchase Agreement (the Contract) is entered into by and between _____, hereinafter referred to as "Buyer" and _____with a mailing address of _____,
hereinafter referred to as "Seller".

Property. Seller hereby agrees to sell the agreed upon property located at _____ (The

Property) to Buyer, who hereby agrees to purchase this property with all structures currently on the premises including all improvements, fixtures, and appurtenances thereon or incidental thereto.

Purchase Price.

The purchase price of this property to be paid at close of escrow by the Buyer in the amount of $_____.
The purchase price shall be paid to the seller as follows:

An Earnest Money Deposit (EMD) of $_____.

The remaining sum of $_____ at close of escrow.

When escrow closes, the earnest money deposit in escrow shall be credited towards the purchase price. If this contract is cancelled by Buyer pursuant to the terms of this contract, Buyer becomes entitled to a return of the earnest money deposit and the escrow agent shall immediately refund to Buyer all earnest money deposits then in escrow together with all interest thereon, if any.

Close of Escrow. The closing date shall occur on or before 30 days from execution of this contract (COE date). COE shall occur when exclusive physical possession is given to Buyer, and the deed is recorded at the appropriate county recorder's office. Buyer and Seller agree to comply with all terms and conditions of this contract, execute and deliver to the assigned escrow agent all closing documents, and perform all other acts necessary for COE to occur. Buyer shall have the right to approve the property's title status before COE. Title to the property shall be conveyed to Buyer at COE by a general warranty deed or equivalent warranty deed used in the local jurisdiction. Buyer shall take title as determined by Buyer before the COE.

Property Turnover. Seller will provide Buyer with keys and any remotes to the property and vacate the property by 12:00 A.M. PST on COE. All personal property left on site, either within the residence or on the property grounds, will transfer with the property and will become the property of the Buyer upon COE.

Inspection Period. Buyer's obligations to close this transaction are subject to the satisfaction of the following conditions on or 24 hours before COE.

(1) Buyer is satisfied with the status of the title to the Property as disclosed by the title commitment provided to Buyer.

(2) Buyer is satisfied with Buyer's investigations and inspections of the property and with the results of the Buyer's physical inspection of the property. In that regard, Buyer shall have ___3___ days (Inspection Period) prior to COE during which time Buyer will have the absolute right to cancel this contract, at Buyer's sole and absolute discretion. Upon such cancellation, Buyer shall be entitled to a return of earnest money deposits.

Investor Disclosure. Buyer is an investor and purchases properties with the intent to lease, resell, or otherwise make a profit. Seller acknowledges that the purchase price may be less than market value, and is willingly selling it at the agreed-upon purchase price for convenience, time savings, lack of funds to renovate, and/or personal reasons. Buyer has not made Seller any representations or promises to the value of the Property. The property is being purchased in its "As Is" condition as of the execution date of this contract.

Remedies. If Seller fails to comply with any provision of this contract than Seller will be considered in breach of this contract. Breach of contract entitles Buyer to pursue any and all remedies available to the Buyer including specific performance. Seller agrees to pay reasonable court costs and attorney fees if a breach occurs.

Representations by Seller. Seller represents and warrants to Buyer as follows:

This contract and each of the documents and agreements to be delivered by the Seller at COE constitute legal, valid, and binding obligations of Seller. These obligations are enforceable against Seller in accordance with their respective terms.

Neither the execution of this contract nor the performance by Seller of its obligations under this contract will result in any breach or violation to Seller's knowledge, of 1) the terms of any law, rule, ordinance, or regulation; or 2) any decree, judgment, or order to which Seller is a party now in effect from any court or governmental body; and 3) there are no consents, waivers, authorizations, or approvals from any third party necessary to be obtained by the Seller in order to carry out the transactions contemplated by this contract.

The payoff of the total of all loans and other debts and encumbrances secured against the property is approximately $_____.

Each of the representations and warranties of the Seller contained in this section constitutes a material part of the consideration to Buyer. Buyer is relying on the accuracy and completeness of the statements and warranties represented in this contract. Each of the designated statements and warranties is true and accurate as of the date of this contract's execution and will be valid and correct as of COE and will survive COE.

Other Agreements. Seller shall not sign nor give verbal commitment to enter into any contract to sell, lease, option or rent with anyone else concerning the property from the execution of this contract. Seller has not signed any other contracts and has the legal right to sell the property.

Vacation of Property. Seller shall vacate the property on or before COE.

Escrow Charges and Closing Costs. Upon COE, Buyer agrees to pay all normal, non-reoccurring escrow fees to the title company and recording fees and/or Attorney fees. Specific fees incurred by the Seller or the Buyer are the responsibility of that party if they are not considered to be part of the normal, non-reoccurring escrow fees to the title company and recording fees.

Agency. Seller acknowledges that Seller has not been represented by any agent or broker with respect to the purchase and sale of the property. Seller agrees and acknowledges that Buyer and representatives of Buyer are not acting as Seller's broker or agent in this transaction. Any and all actions by Buyer and representatives of the Buyer have been acted solely for Buyer's benefit as a principle of this contract. Seller acknowledges that Buyer is not a licensed real estate agent or brokerage. Seller understands there are licensed real estate professionals either employed or contracted by the Buyer, including Realtors, Appraisers, Loan Officers, etc., however, this does not constitute any type of representation to the Seller. Seller agrees to hold the Buyer and its representatives (both employed and contracted) free from any and all liability regarding this property and transactions arising from any claim of the agency.

Existing Financing. Seller shall satisfy any and all monetary liens on the property as of COE. Buyer acknowledges that if the actual payoff figure is higher than the sum represented by Seller herein that the transaction may not be feasible to Seller. In the event of the sum being higher than what was represented, Buyer reserves the right to cancel this contract.

Assignment and Release. Seller agrees and acknowledges that Buyer may assign its rights under this agreement to a wholly or partially owned entity of Buyer or a third party that will close directly with Seller.

Condemnation and Casualty. Seller bears all risk of loss until COE. Buyer may terminate this contract and obtain a refund of the earnest money deposit if improvements on the property are destroyed or materially damaged before COE. Alternatively, Buyer may elect to proceed with closing, in which case, at COE Seller shall assign to Buyer all claims and rights to proceeds under any affected insurance policy and shall credit Buyer at COE the amount of any deductible provided for the policy. Seller and Buyer may also mutually choose to extend closing to allow Seller to fix/repair/replace any items of material damage.

Prorations. Real property taxes and HOA monthly fees payable by Seller will be prorated to COE. The amount of any assessment, other than homeowner's association assessments, that is a lien as of COE shall be paid in full by the Seller. Any current rents will be prorated as well with Seller agreeing to provide documents as requested from Escrow Coordinator. Any security deposits will be transferred from Seller to Buyer at COE.

Expiration. This offer to purchase expires on _____ .

Additional Terms and Conditions. (If none, write none)

_____

_____.

Seller Signature _____ Date _____

Seller Printed Name _____

Buyer Signature _____ Date _____

Buyer Printed Name _____

    No matter which contract you choose, either one of these or one of your own, really only works when you understand the contract and you can explain it and sell it as well. Don't be afraid to adjust your contract to close a deal. We recently had a deal where the seller would only sign if we added the comment in the additional terms "Seller to Net $30,000." We had already based our price on the Seller netting this amount, so it really was already covered, but sometimes the seller gets what the seller wants. What happens if we get to the closing table and the seller is only getting $28,714, and they demand we pay them the remaining $1,286? Well, if it is a really good deal for us, we would pay it, but in this case we prepped the Seller ahead of time by letting them know the contract price was above what we were willing to pay initially, which makes it easier to swallow getting "almost $30,000." You have to be prepared for negotiations throughout the contract. Even though you lay out terms and they are signed, you will be contacted by sellers throughout the transaction with questions about many different things. We have bought cell phones for sellers, helped them move, rented back to them, bought them cigarettes, raised prices, lowered prices, bought vehicles, we've even bailed them out of jail! No matter what problems come up, find a solution!

Are these contracts perfect? No. If you put them in front of a lawyer, will the lawyer want to make changes? Yes. There isn't a lawyer alive who likes a contract they didn't create (and charge for). Do I get deals from these contracts? Yes. If you are missing something from your contracts, or the wording isn't correct or fully understood at closing, you have to realize that your escrow company is there to help you. They can facilitate additional paperwork if needed, ranging from adding sellers, to extensions of escrow, to changes in price, and so on. They are working with both you and the seller to get this property closed, and they are there to help. Lean on your team for assistance. A good title and escrow agent is worth their weight in gold, and you will lean on their expertise to help you close more deals. Don't be afraid to ask questions when you don't know the answers.

Additionally, if you don't like these contracts, you don't have to use them. I'm not a lawyer, and by no means are my comments or any of the contracts herein meant to be legal advice of any sort, but I can say that I have closed deals with both of the contracts above. Maybe you have a contract someone in your market has already shared with you, or maybe you have paid thousands of dollars for a course and they supplied you with a contract. That is fine, use what you are comfortable with and can help you convince the seller to sign, because that is really the goal here. Get the seller to sign.

No matter what contract you use, there are going to be a few blanks that you are going to have to fill in. So let's run through those.

- Seller. This is the person or persons (or even entity) who is the recorded owner on title. All sellers will have to sign the contract. If a husband and wife are both on the title, both will have to sign. Most entities (LLCs, Corporations, Trusts, and so on) will have one approved signer and that will be sufficient.

- Purchase price. This is either the agreed upon price, or the price you are presenting to the seller.

- EMD. The earnest money deposit will really depend on you and your bankroll. I know some wholesalers who only do $10. I recommend $100 minimum and more if you can afford it. I do $5,000 for my EMDs. Why? Because if I am going up against another wholesaler who offered $10, I am now the more legitimate buyer.

- Close of Escrow. The longer the better, because it gives you more time to sell your deal to the end buyer. We typically do thirty days for the closing, but let the seller know we may be able to close earlier depending on inspections, and title work and lien releases.

- Buyer signature. That's you. You are the buyer on the purchase contract. The seller is the seller and you are the buyer ... for now. The goal for you is to then assign the right to purchase through an assignment agreement. That is another contract that you will sign later, once you find the end buyer.

That is basically it. Don't be afraid of contracts. Keep them simple and only use contracts that you understand and can help you close the deals. But remember, without a contract signed by both you and a seller, you don't have a deal. Get those signatures and make sure to always have a copy of every contract you sign.

CASH MORE CHECKS

- Use contracts that you understand.

- If you don't know something, ask!

- A contract should help you close deals, not hurt it.

- Sometimes a seller gets what a seller wants.

- Get those signatures, there is no deal if there is no signature.

- Always keep copies of your paperwork, you will need them!

CHAPTER 8

You've Got the Contract, Now What?

Congratulations, you have a signed contract with a seller. Now what? Now the fun begins, and it all happens at the same time. First and foremost, if either you or your representative hasn't visited the property yet, you need to make this happen. Get out to the property and take a lot of photos, not just fifteen or twenty, but 100 or 150. This is for two reasons: to share with your buyers, but also to possibly negotiate a lower price with your seller if your inspection leads to finding the property was not in the condition the seller said it was in. A good picture can help reduce a sales price by thousands, especially for an out-of-town seller.

While you are scheduling your inspection, you will also want to open escrow. You will email your contract to your desired title/escrow company or attorney (depending on your state, some areas close with title companies or with closing attorneys). Send them the fully signed (fully executed) contract and be prepared to wire the EMD you agreed to as well. Typically, this needs to be done in the first two days after opening escrow.

Once escrow is opened, the title officer or attorney will do their research on the property to make sure the property can be sold, to make sure the correct owner is selling it, and to find out how much is owed on the property for items like bank loans, past-due taxes, contractor liens, and so on.

Your inspection can be done by anyone: a Realtor, a contractor, your mom, Joe, or you. You don't have to be an expert at construction or building to do what is needed here. You are just going to the property, let the seller or tenant know you are going to walk through and take some photographs, and check the condition of the mechanicals. The mechanicals are the heating and air conditioners, the water heater, the pool equipment, and the electric panel. These aren't invasive inspections with special equipment and gauges, you are keeping it simple. If it is hot out, is it cold inside because the air conditioning is on? Yes? Great, the AC works. No? Ask the person who opened the door for you about the AC, they'll probably tell you it's broken. Test the water. How? Turn on a few faucets and flush a toilet. Keep it simple. When you do find items that are not working, take pictures, both up close and far away from them. You don't just want pictures up close of a missing showerhead, you also want the picture of the entire bathroom. Again, it doesn't have to be invasive, you don't have to shimmy under the crawl space or dig through someone's attic. You are just getting enough information to send out to your buyers. Is the house in good shape? Okay shape? Needs some updating? Bad shape? Real buyers will buy based on these descriptions, and a decent set of photographs lets your buyer know if it is a good, fair, bad, or ugly.

If the property is rented, during this time you will also want to get a copy of the lease if one exists and verify the rent amount with both the seller and renter, if possible. If a property is transferring with a tenant, nine times out of ten your buyer will want a copy of that lease.

Additional questions your buyers may ask you if a property is rented and that you should be prepared to answer:

- Is rent paid to date?

- Is there a history, a ledger, of rent payments?

- Is there a written lease?

- Is the tenant wanting to stay or are they prepared to move?

- Has the eviction process started? (that's if the tenant is paying rent)

- How much time is left on the lease

- Is there a security deposit and will that transfer with the property?

- Who pays current utilities?

The more prepared you are to answer the questions of your buyer, the quicker you will be able to sell your wholesale properties.

If, during your inspection you see any documents that might be important, ranging from a lease to a notice from the city posted on the building, make sure to take very good, clear pictures of the paperwork. The more information you have and the more thorough you are at the front of the transaction, the easier it will be to communicate this information to the buyer.

That's right, don't forget, you still have to work the other half of this transaction. You've done the A to B portion of it, the A being the seller and you being B, the wholesaler or assignor. Now you have to work the B to C portion of this wholesale deal and get yourself a buyer.

CASH MORE CHECKS

- Once that contract is signed, do everything!

- Keep it simple. If it works, it works.

- Good photographs are the best way to sell your deal.

- Don't be afraid to renegotiate if the property isn't what the seller described.

- Get copies of all of the paperwork.

- Do things right, so you don't have to do them a second time.

CHAPTER 9

How Do You Move Your Product?

Buyers are the key to growing your real estate whole-saling business and moving your product. Without buyers, there is no deal. Where do you find real buyers? Everywhere, honestly. I've already named a few ways throughout this book. In fact, if you took action when I told you to earlier in this book by placing the ghost ad, you may already have buyers contacting you. Check your email right now. That's right, put this book down and check your email to see if you have any responses. If not, place another ad. This time I want you to do two ghost ads in two different markets, one in your local real estate market and one in the biggest city in the state next to you (sorry Hawaii and Alaska, you'll just have to pick a state at random). Go ahead, I'll wait while you do it. And again, if you are telling yourself *I'll do it later* or blowing this off, why are you reading this book? Take action! That is how you start and grow your business. You have a phone sitting next to you, in your pocket, or maybe you already have it in your hands because you are reading this book on it. Post!

All right, let's get back to where else you can find buyers. And I mean real buyers, not just those people who went to a seminar or watched a video on YouTube or read a book (ha, ha). Where do you find the buyers who are currently buying and have access to plenty of money? I'm talking about the buyers with five-million-dollar credit lines, stacks of private investors, and an infrastructure that needs to be fed so they buy more property. Well, it's really not that difficult, if you know where to look and who to ask.

Before we get into the where to look and who to ask, I want you to do another task. Yes, even though I just told you to post some ads. This time I want you to go on to Facebook and, if you haven't yet done so, I want you to join at a minimum five new wholesaling groups. You can find groups local to your market, but the bigger ones will be national ones and can have more than twenty-five thousand members in them. Go into these five groups and write a post that says something like "I'm looking for a wholesale-friendly title company/closing agent in (your city)." Now hopefully you understand that you need to pick your city and type it in the parenthesis. Do this in five separate groups. Use a colored background in two of the posts, and for the other three posts I want you to "check in" in your city, so it shows a map. This will help make the post stand out more instead of it just being a simple word post. Once you are done with that, come on back to the book. I'll wait.

Okay, hopefully you are done with your posts and didn't just keep reading, because if you did that, you are just cheating yourself. Again, if you want to be successful in this business you have to take action. Now, back to real buyers and where you find them. The real key to knowing if someone is a real buyer is by seeing if they are actually buying. Anyone can talk a real big game and make it sound like they are buying five to ten properties per month, but unless you have proof, it isn't real. So let's get into the best ways to find buyers!

Track other Wholesaler's Deals. It's going to be important for you to sign up as a Buyer on every other wholesaler's list that you can find in your market area. That way, you can track their deals and follow to see who actually ends up buying them (if they even sell). Keep a list of these deals and review them once a month to see if they closed. If they closed, record the buyer's name and the sale price. This process will take time, but over the course of a few months you will end up seeing some names over and over again and, if you are in a disclosure state, you will have the buyer's name and address. At that point, it is as simple as writing them a letter (yes, an actual snail mail letter with a stamp and envelope) stating that you wholesale real estate in their market and would like to add them to your buyers list. Now you aren't looking for a pen pal, so make sure you include your phone number and email address for them to contact you, and if you have a link to your website where they can sign in and be added to your buyers list, even better!

Additionally, as these deals come over, you may be inspired by the way they present their deals, what software they are using, how they do photo links, and so on. You can learn from others by watching what they do. (Additionally, this can be a source of future deals for you, too. If this lead never closes and falls out of contract, guess what? Now you have a new lead on an owner wanting to sell.

Leads from Escrow Agents. Those last posts you put on Facebook, asking for a wholesale-friendly title company?

Remember those? The ones you actually did? Well, those are used to find contacts within your marketplace that can link you up with actual buyers. Chances are that if someone responded to your post with a title company or closing agent, that person has used them before to close a wholesale deal and that agent probably closes deals with other wholesalers, flippers, and investors throughout the market area. I know that when I do wholesale deals or flips, I have my preferred agents and, over time, they typically end up getting busier and busier because every deal I do adds another client to their portfolio! If they are good, people keep coming back to them and want to refer them to others. So, what do you do? You reach out to them, and it's best to do so by email. If you have their name and company name, it's usually just a simple Google search to find their email address. Send them an email and let them know that they were recommended to you as being a go-to escrow agent for investors. Tell them you have a deal and if they have any of their preferred investors they should share your contact information with them, that way the investor can contact you directly. Notice you aren't asking them to give up their client information, you are asking them to share your information with their client. That way, it is their client's choice to contact you or not. I actually get multiple leads every month from escrow agents this way, either from Realtors or investors who have deals falling out, and my closing agents know that I can get deals closed, either by being the buyer or by bringing a different buyer to the table. Why would an escrow agent do this? First, it helps their numbers by doing more closings and secondly, it builds loyalty with their top-closing clients. That's right, typically they won't refer you to the investor who is only doing one deal every couple of months. They will refer you to the investor who is doing multiple deals every single month. It builds loyalty. The more we can help each other, the better it is for everyone. Proven buyers are great buyers.

Auctions. Go to your local auctions, either for taxes or foreclosures, and see who the buyers are there. Pay attention to the bidding, and you will see a few people who just bid on one property and bid low. Chances are, though, if you stick around for the entire auction or go regularly for a few weeks, you will see a few repeat bidders bidding on most of the inventory. Most of the time, these are buyers for hedge funds. For a simple definition, a hedge fund is a Wall Street group with a lot of money that needs to invest in a lot of assets. Many of these hedge funds have pockets that start with a "B," as in billion. Don't interrupt their bidding, but when the auction is over, go up to them and ask if they buy from wholesalers. If they say yes, ask if they have a card to put them on your buyers list. Don't be offended if they say they don't, as I know some of them are pretty strict on their buying criteria including how they purchase inventory. The auctions are also just a great place to network. Talk to other people who are there, pay attention to the list that is being auctioned, and run your numbers on the properties. It will help you get the pulse of the buyer base in your immediate market area. If there are a lot of bidders, it's a hot market. If there aren't many bidders and properties aren't selling, it's a slow market.

Tax/Assessor Records. If you are in a disclosure state that actually posts and records the sale of real estate in public records, you can do a monthly search and look for repeat buyers. Many times this will be an online database that you can search and possibly even sort. If you see the same names show-ing up, typically this will be a business name ending with "LLC," as that is what most professional buyers purchase through, this most likely is an investor you want to target. Again, send them a snail mail letter with your contact info and a link to your site so they can sign up. Or, just send them your phone number and email, stating you would like to schedule a time to talk to them about their buying criteria and what type of properties they would like you to send them.

Those are my top four favorite ways to find buyers directly and they work best when you are in the market and doing mul-tiple deals there. You don't need a list of one hundred or one thousand buyer names, because most likely ninety-five percent of those lists aren't even real buyers. They are just other whole-salers, Realtors, or new investors who are not going to pull the trigger. The goal of this is to find five to ten real buyers. But you shouldn't just look at them as buyers, you should look at them as additional team members.

So how do you tell if someone is a real buyer once you have started interacting with them? Well, there are multiple ways. A real buyer typically doesn't need an extensive amount of infor-mation from you. When I am buying from wholesalers, I tell them all I need is:

1. The Address

2. Pictures

3. My price

So, what do you as a wholesaler need to send?

The Address. That's pretty easy and straightforward, but I honestly see wholesalers send the wrong address so many times it doesn't even surprise me any more. Take some time and some pride in what you are doing. Additionally, if you send the correct, full address without any typos or transposed numbers, you will cut out multiple follow-up emails, which will save you time. Time is your most valuable asset, so don't waste it.

Pictures. Don't text people fifty pictures or email them in four or five separate emails. Get a Dropbox account or a Google Drive account where you can upload fifty to one hundred and fifty pictures of the property, and then share a link to the folder. Again, it will save you time and make it easier for your buyer to make a quick decision.

My Price. I get questioned on this all the time, what does my price mean? If a buyer is asking for that, they just want to know how much you are selling the deal for. They don't want to know how much you have it under contract for or how much your assignment fee is. Never present a deal by saying "I have it under contract for $150,000 and would like to make $10,000, so will you buy it for $160,000?" No. If you do that, I will slap you. Seriously. Don't do that. If you want a $10,000 assignment fee, just tell your buyer, "The deal is available for $160,000." They don't need all of the other details to make their decision.

Now this is very important and you should really pay attention to this one. My wife, who is on my team, is one of the best negotiators I have ever known. She has a motto, "You don't ask people what they want, you tell them what you want."

Now, this may go against other strategies you have read or been taught. I know plenty of wholesalers who present their deals to their buyers with just an address and pictures, maybe they put their ARV and a brief description of the property in an email, and then they take bids on the properties for twenty-four or forty-eight hours. I don't like this as a business model, because you will lose buyers who don't want to look at your deals and play games. For a buyer, this is like playing darts blindfolded. If I, as a buyer, see a deal come over like this with no asking price, I don't even research it anymore because I don't want to waste my time. Remember, time is your most valuable asset and the most valuable asset of your buyers, too. I used to make offers on everything, even when wholesalers would send a deal with no price. For the numbers to even be close, I would have to buy at $150,000 and they would come back and tell me things like, "Sorry, it won't work, I have it under contract at $185,000." If they had put in their email or text they wanted $195,000 or $200,000, I would have looked at the email and in ten seconds known that I wasn't even remotely interested in that deal. That's right, a good buyer will be able to see the zip code, a few pictures of the house and the house size, and based on their experience will be able to smell test it as a potential deal or not. I don't want to waste five minutes of my day chasing your bad deal. And guess what, I don't make offers on the deals of those wholesalers anymore. Yes, they could have a deal in the future, but guess what? I, as a buyer, am getting deals from lots of wholesalers, realtors, homeowners, auctions, and on and on. I, as a buyer, don't need your wholesale deal and that is the attitude of real buyers once you have wasted their time multiple times.

So why do some wholesalers use this strategy? Because on some deals they can make larger assignment fees, especially in

Luko Wobor

hot markets. I don't want to discount it because I don't like this method, because yes, it can make you some extra money on a deal sometimes. If you put your deal out to your buyers list, which you can do through most real estate CRMs, and send it with:

1. Address

2. Pictures

3. ARV

4. Comparable sales (you will cherry pick the best ones to show a higher ARV)

5. A brief description of the property

6. Starting bid, auction time, or a line like "Taking offers until 5 p.m. tomorrow"

With that sixth line, you may get bids. You may have hoped to sell a property for $160,000, but somebody might come in and pay you $170,000 for it. Now instead of a $10,000 assignment fee, you are collecting $20,000. That's great, right? But if you ran your numbers right, you know that this buyer most likely is paying too much for the deal. If they pay too much for this deal, and especially if they lose money on the deal when it is done, they won't buy from you again. And that is the true caveat here, because what is your most valuable asset? Time. Wouldn't you rather send one text or email message to a group of five or ten buyers, the first one who replies "I'll take it" at your listed price and bam, you have a buyer and a deal locked up? Or would you like to create an auction atmosphere on every deal you do, try out new buyers on almost every single closing,

119

not knowing if they will move forward, be able to close, back out without putting in EMD, and so on? I see this a lot when people do auction-style listings. Many times that deal hits the open market again and again, or the original buyer who said they would take $170,000 can't get funding for the deal because the hard money lender or private investor they were going to use to fund the deal ran their numbers and said it wasn't a deal, so now that guy backs out, you go back to your next highest bid that may have been $160,000 and ask her if she wants it. She is smart enough to know she has the power now and says, "After further research I can only do $155,000 on it." Tables have turned on you, you are running out of time on your contract, and you have to just take her offer and move forward with it. What could have been a $10,000 assignment fee has now dropped to a $5,000 assignment fee and you created ten times more work for yourself. Could you have found another deal in that time? Maybe. When I wholesale deals, I give a price that I want someone to pay and I think is reasonable for the market, I don't ask them how much they want to pay.

I am just trying to give you as much information as possible, because ultimately it is your business. I know wholesalers all across the country who are very successful using both of these methods for selling their deals. I personally view this as a relationship business, and I want my buyers to be repeat buyers and be successful. I give them a price, and if the number works for them we both win. As a buyer, I have even bought bad deals (something with very little end profit) from wholesalers just so they could move inventory and I could hopefully get their next good one. As a flipper or as a wholesaler, I always play the long game.

I have helped a lot of wholesalers in my market grow their businesses by educating them, directing them, and most importantly buying from them, and this is what a good buyer will do. They want to see you succeed. I have wholesalers who will send me an address and ask me what number I need to be at to purchase it, even prior to them getting it under contract. If I was unethical, I could go around them and track the deal down myself, but why would I do that? I view these wholesalers as members of my team. Additionally, if they can find one deal, most likely they can find more.

CASH MORE CHECKS

- Understand your buyers.

- Time is your best resource.

- Auction or set price? You decide.

- Repeat buyers are the best buyers.

- Tell them what you want, don't ask what they want.

- Don't let other people count your money.

- More buyers equals more opportunity

CHAPTER 10

Assigning and Closing—Your Fee Is Never too Big

Once you have a property under contract, you've completed all of your inspections and due diligence, you have found a Buyer, and they agree to buy your interest in your Real Estate Purchase Agreement (remember, you aren't selling a property, you are selling your interest, your rights to purchase a property), you still need to do more paperwork! Yes, everything should be in writing and, as with any contract you are using, you should understand what it says. Below is the assignment agreement that we use. It's basic and straightforward.

Agreement to Assign Rights to
Purchase Contract

Subject Property Address: _____

This Agreement is made between _____
_____ (ASSIGNOR) and _____
_____ (ASSIGNEE) regarding the Purchase Contract of the above referenced SUBJECT PROPERTY with a contract date of _____.

Whereas Assignor has entered into a Purchase Contract as the Buyer with _____
(SELLER) for the purchase of the SUBJECT PROPERTY, and whereas Assignor wishes to assign its rights, interests, and obligations in the Purchase Contract, it is hereby agreed between ASSIGNOR and ASSIGNEE as follows:

a. ASSIGNEE shall pay ASSIGNOR a NON-REFUNDABLE Assignment Fee of $_____ (to be wired to Title/Escrow within 24 hours from the date of this mutually executed agreement). If clear title cannot be provided, Assignee may cancel this Agreement and receive a full refund of the Assignment Fee. Assignee acknowledges they have completed their due diligence and have not relied on Assignor in their decision-making process regarding condition, value, property characteristics, etc. Assignor makes no warranty, either written or implied, regarding value, condition, etc. At closing, Assignor shall receive the Assignment fee and any earnest money deposit previously deposited.

b. Assignor reserves the right to continue to market this Agreement until Assignor has received confirmation the Assignment Fee has been received by Title/Escrow.

c. Assignee's inspection period shall expire upon execution of this Agreement. ASSIGNEE accepts all terms and conditions of the contract for Sale and Purchase between BUYER and SELLER in its entirety.

d. ASSIGNEE acknowledges receipt of legible copies of the original Purchase Contract in its entirety and ASSIGNEE agrees to close the Purchase transaction on or before _____.

e. This Agreement is non-assignable without the express written consent of the ASSIGNOR. No changes to the Purchase Contract can be made without written Consent of Assignor. Assignee will not attempt to renegotiate the original Purchase Contract, any attempts to do so will forfeit the Assignment Fee and Assignor may cancel this Agreement if they so choose.

AGREED AND ACCEPTED

_____

Assignor Signature _____Date _____

Assignee Signature _____Date _____

After reading the contract, you should have noticed a couple of things. You are the Assignor and you are getting a non-refundable fee from the Assignee. The Assignee is the end buyer that you found. Now a few things could happen when you send this to your buyer and they see your actual fee. Remember, your fee is the difference between the contract price you agreed on with the seller and the price you agreed on with the buyer. If you signed the original contract for $250,000 and your buyer said they could pay $270,000 for the property, that is a $20,000 assignment fee and that is what you input into the assignment agreement, not $270,000. Some buyers will congratulate you for making $20,000 and others will be upset. Don't let other people count your money! They don't know what you had to go through to get this deal, they don't know how much you had to pay in marketing, or if you had to pay off a credit card bill for the seller. Don't let others count your money. If they said $270,000 works for them, then it should still work for them whether you are making $50 assignment fee or a $100,000 assignment fee. Find the buyers who cheer your success and keep working with them.

Additionally, when you send the assignment agreement to the buyer, you will want to send them a copy of the original contract. That way the buyer knows what terms they are actually agreeing to. I have had multiple wholesale deals that I bought from wholesalers and they didn't understand why I requested the contract before I signed the Assignment. A buyer will want to know what they are agreeing to. What if you have a crazy term in your contract such as "Seller will leaseback property for 36 months at $500.00"? I actually had that happen to me on one. This might not have been an issue if the property was being bought for $20,000 and I planned on keeping it as a rental. However, it was a $360,000 property that had a market rent of $2,800 and I planned on flipping it. Always make sure you know and understand what you are signing.

Once the assignment agreement is executed (signed by both you and the new buyer), you need to send a copy of the agreement to your title/escrow company along with the new buyer's contact information. Title/escrow will reach out to the new buyer with wiring instructions to send their assignment fee. Remember, per the agreement this is due within twenty-four hours from execution of the contract. If they don't put this money in, they lose the deal and you can sell to someone else.

Now where is your money? You have your purchase contract signed with the seller and you have your assignment agreement with the buyer. When do you get paid? You get paid when the deal actually closes. That means you had better babysit this deal all the way through to the end. Keep talking with the seller and keep talking with the buyer. Make sure everyone is doing what they need to do. Make sure they go to the title company on the day of closing so they can sign their final closing paperwork. Make sure the buyer wires their money to escrow (I prefer they do this the day before the scheduled closing). Closing day is the exciting day. This is when the buyer performs on their end, they get their money to the title/escrow company, and the property changes ownership from the seller to the buyer. The title/escrow company will disburse all of the funds to the appropriate party. If the seller had a mortgage, the title/escrow company will wire them their funds. If the seller had any equity, the title/escrow company will wire them their funds. If the buyer had a refund coming, the title/escrow company will wire them their funds. So what about you? Yes, the title/escrow company will send you your funds, too! Now remember, you aren't just going to be getting your assignment fee, you will also be getting the EMD back too. How do you want it? Do you want it at closing or do you want to wait seven days for it? That's right, that is the basic difference between getting the funds wired to your bank account like everyone else or swinging by the title company and picking up a check. I do a lot of closings, and I don't have the time to swing by the title company and I also like my money now. I always get wires. However, if you want to post a big fat check on social media, you can. Take a copy of it and use it as motivation. But will a picture of that check get you more deals? No, your time will. Get your money and keep your next deals moving forward.

CASH MORE CHECKS

- Force your buyers to act. If they don't wire their money, they don't get the deal.

- Keep marketing until the contract is signed AND the EMD is in.

- Your assignment fee is never too big.

- Don't count someone else's money and don't let them count yours.

- Communication closes deals.

- You get paid when the deal closes, so make sure it closes.

CHAPTER 11

Virtual Wholesaling and Joint Ventures
(Beware the Daisy Chain)

If you've already been playing around in various Facebook groups or other social media hubs, you have probably already seen the term "Virtual Wholesaling." What this means is that you are doing all of the items listed in this book, but at a distance. You are doing it virtually. You are doing it from just a phone and a computer. You are never walking the property, you are never shaking hands with the owner, and you are never meeting your buyer face to face. To wholesale virtually, you really have to be an expert on the phones, because you are going to have to lean on other individuals for a lot of information and you are going to have to be able to convince them to get it for you.

Let's start out with the basics of the property and I'll tell you my preferred methods to get what I want.

Pictures. Anybody can get pictures, but you want to get the right pictures. I don't just tell someone "send me some pictures of your house." I tell them to get me two pictures of the front, two of the kitchen, two of each bathroom, and one or two of each of the other rooms, depending on the size. Additionally, send me any pictures of anything you think adds value to the home or has been recently replaced, as well as any pictures of current damage. I let them know that I want to be able to make my best offer the first time, and if I have more data, it typically leads to a higher and more accurate offer. If the seller doesn't live in the house, I ask them to have their tenant do it. If the owner lives away from the property, I contact a local Realtor, and through the owner schedule a time for the Realtor to walk the property. There are even services you can pay to go take photographs in most major cities across the United States, but do this as a last resort.

Comparable Sales. Just like we discussed in Chapter 5, there are multiple resources available to find comparable sales, but I still prefer to talk to local Realtors who understand the nuances of a marketplace and what a property can and can't sell for. Get on the phone or send emails to local Realtors. Let them know you are buying a property and need some help determining what it can sell for. But be careful, as some Realtors will go around you and try to get it as a listing straight from the seller. It's best to reach out to Realtors after you have it under contract. I also like to dangle the carrot with these Realtors, letting them know that I have this property, but others coming up as well. If the Realtor thinks there is more work, and in turn more commissions for them, coming down the road, they will be more likely to help you upfront. Realtors make commission when they sell properties, typically 3% of the sales price. If they think they might get a listing from you, or possibly some free leads, they should be willing to help you with comparable sale searches based on that future income. If you get a Realtor that wants to charge you upfront for this service, move on. Once you find a good Realtor or two, you can really develop this into a win-win situation. I've had Realtors that have pulled comparable sales from me even send me leads that I later either closed or wholesaled. Connect with more real estate professionals and stay connected with the ones that you can grow with.

Condition. I know multiple wholesalers who actually pay for home inspections on properties. This is a licensed individual who goes into a property, does a full inspection to find out what is working and what is not, writes up a report (with pictures), and sends it to you. One of the great things about this method is that if you find multiple items of repair needed, now you have that information from a disinterested third party and you can use that to get a price reduction from the seller. These typically cost between two and four hundred dollars, and price will depend on size and location of the property.

And that's about it. Pictures, comparables, and condition, otherwise everything is pretty much the same as doing it in person. You can sign documents with an electronic signature program like Docusign or Hellosign. Upload your contract as a PDF, mark the fields you want signed and dated, and email it to your seller and buyers! We even use digital signatures on our local deals because it is such a great tool. You truly can do this business from anywhere.

Now you may be asking what is a joint venture or co-wholesaling as some people call it? After you start joining more Facebook groups or listening to more gurus, you are going to see a lot on this. To put it bluntly, joint ventures are the easy way out. Now that doesn't necessarily mean that it is a bad thing, but there are definitely bad ways to do it. Let's be very clear here, a joint venture is not the same as a daisy chain. A daisy chain is bad, and typically a waste of everyone's time. You may post one of your wholesale deals and a buyer shows up and makes you an offer, signs the assignment agreement, and now that they control it, they market it out to other buyers for a few thousand more. They didn't have to do the front-end work and are now trying to skim a couple grand off of it, but so much gets lost in translation, they aren't upfront about it, there are multiple parties involved and each is being told different things, and in the end these rarely work out and you just end up with a very angry seller and no money. I've seen daisy chains that have had four different parties involved on them, with each trying to make a chunk of money! This is one of the reasons you need to get on every wholesaler's list in your market area, so you can find out if someone is out there trying to shop your deal to other buyers.

Now a joint venture (JV) is similar to a daisy chain, but it should be done with upfront honesty. Either the contract holder or another wholesaler who saw the deal can initiate a joint venture. When I have a contract in a market I am not familiar with, I do like to reach out to other wholesalers I see who are very active in the marketplace. I'll find someone who is responsive and can even be used as my boots on the ground for pictures and inspections. I'll set terms with the local wholesaler, my joint venture partner, and these will not be the terms I have with the seller. For example, if I have a property under contract for $60,000 and I know it should be able to be assigned for $80,000 to $90,000 based on sales data and my formula, I will tell my JV partner that I will split anything I get over

$75,000 with them fifty/fifty. If they are able to move it to their buyer database for $80,000, they will get a quick $2,500 and I will get $17,500. You can do your splits however you want, split the entire assignment fee fifty/fifty or give a flat rate if they find a buyer, there really is no right or wrong way to do this. Well, I guess the only wrong way to do this is to try to cheat the other side out of their cut. If someone brings you a buyer, pay them. If someone brings you a deal to joint venture on, don't try to steal their contract. Remember, this is a relationship business and in this day and age of social media, you don't want to build a bad reputation for yourself. And anyways, being honest is just the right thing to do.

Remember, daisy chains are bad. They are built on dishonesty and lead to poor communication and deals not closing. Joint ventures are open and honest and are built around teamwork. You may ask yourself, *Why would someone even daisy chain a deal or want to do a joint venture?* Many people want to get into the business of wholesaling real estate, but they aren't closers with sellers, they don't know how to market, they are afraid of contracts, or they just listened to the wrong guru who told them this is the easiest and a less-risky way to make money. Let me put it like this, the ones who are daisy chaining deals are going to McDonald's and buying a cheeseburger, then going out and selling that cheeseburger to someone in the parking lot. They don't want to make the burger, they don't know how to grill it or season it, and they don't know how to put the condiments on correctly. Can this work? Yes, but there isn't much markup to be had on a twice-purchased burger. Wouldn't you rather know how to cook the burger and get your own clients? That is where the real money is.

Now the burger story is more to the people out there who are doing daisy chains. Joint ventures, when done correctly, can be a nice little side business for you, since they create some extra revenue without the added cost of more marketing. Establish yourself as one of the top wholesalers in your market, and other wholesalers will bring you deals to help move.

I recently had a lead come in located in Houston. Since I am based out of Las Vegas, it's not as if I am going to drive that far just for a lead. My team did our research, looking on websites like iComps and Zillow, and found out that the ARV of the property was in the $180,000 range. We contacted the owner, had a discussion, were told the property needed minimal repairs, and they were just tired of managing the rental from a distance (that was their motivation to sell). We assumed a basic cosmetic flip, a Good-condition property, and made an offer to them of $84,500. We sent them the contract and they signed it. Within our contract, we had an inspection period and made the offer contingent upon us inspecting the property. We reached out to our database of other wholesalers in Houston. Some replied, some didn't, and we also looked for new connections. One of these new connections contacted us, he was an experienced wholesaler with a few dozen deals under his belt, and we hit it off. He was willing to go do the inspection for us, he got the photos we needed, sent them in a Dropbox folder, and we reviewed them. After looking at the pictures, we found there were more than just cosmetic repairs needed and we told the seller we needed a lower price due to the roof needing to be replaced and issues with one of the bathroom showers. We asked for the new price to be $70,000, and after some back and forth negotiations we settled on $75,000 and

signed an addendum to the contract. Once the price was rene-
gotiated, we went back to the original wholesale partner and
came to a joint venture agreement with him that we would split
fifty/fifty anything above $85,000 that he could sell the deal for.
He found a buyer at $95,000. He made $5,000 for inspecting a
property for us and linking us up with one of his buyers and
we made $15,000 (the sales price of $95,000 minus the JV partner's $5,000 cut minus the updated contract price of $75,000).
We never walked the property, we never met the seller in person, we never met the JV partner in person, and we never met
the buyer in person (in fact we never even spoke with the end
buyer). All of this was done virtually.

Guess who I am going to call the next time I have another
contract signed in Houston? That's right, this JV partner. Not
his buyer. I am still going to need inspections, I am still going
to need boots on the ground, and I am still going to need an
honest opinion working toward the same goal of selling this
contract. The buyer won't give me those, but this other wholesaler already did and I am confident he will do it again. He
was happy with the transaction, we were happy with the transaction, and the buyer and seller were happy. We even got a
review from the seller. Remember, if you want to go the route
of being the middleman on these transactions, do it with integrity and honesty and get the deals closed, that way you will
get repeat business. These kinds of deals happen every day in
every market around the country and you can be part of them,
close more deals and make more money along the way. In
fact, I know multiple wholesalers who only do joint ventures.
They love being the middleman and they are very good at it,
and there is nothing wrong with that. Instead of focusing on

bringing in leads, they focus on building lists of wholesalers in various market and building lists of buyers in various markets. They have databases with tens of thousands of names of each and when a deal comes in from anywhere in the country, they reach into their database for anyone interested in that market and advertise the deal to them. Some of the bigger outfits I know just tack on or request an additional $2,500 to $5,000 on to the deal for their middleman service. They are upfront and honest about it and have built very successful businesses doing this. A lot of the posts you see on social media of people doing 30+ wholesale deals a month are actually doing a significant amount of these JV deals. It can either be a way to make a little extra money on the side and not let a lead go to waste or it can be a very profitable seven figure business all to its own. No matter which way you utilize, just make sure you are doing it with honesty and integrity.

CASH MORE CHECKS

- Don't daisy chain.

- Joint ventures help both parties.

- A JV can be an entire business by itself.

- If something worked, repeat. Everyone can win together.

- Seller's lie, so trust but verify (and renegotiate that deal!).

- You can do this business from anywhere.

CHAPTER 12

Growing Your Team (And Your Revenue)

Are you a one-person shop? Do you want to stay small and only manage yourself? Close a deal or two a month and live well? Or do you want to go big? Do you want to be a leader, do you want to compete with the companies doing thirty or fifty wholesale deals a month in multiple markets? That will be something you have to decide. There is nothing wrong with either direction, don't think you have to go big to impress someone, and don't think being a one-person show is bad. The one thing you do have to realize is that, as you grow your team, you will need to do more deals as it costs money to keep everyone fed. If you bring on more salespeople to help close more deals, not only will they need to get paid, but you will need to spend more in marketing to get more leads in.

When I am coaching new wholesalers or flippers or even just business owners, I tell them the first thing they should hire out is the thing they don't know how to do or the thing they hate doing the most. For me, it is accounting. I can do it, I just don't like it. Let me hire someone to handle the back end of the business so I can focus on my Income Producing Activities (IPA). Let me close more deals. For you, you may want to hire someone to manage your marketing or someone to manage your transactions and paperwork. Or maybe you want to hire a virtual assistant to make your cold calls. If you are hiring out these positions, make sure that you take the time to train them on what you want them to do and teach them what has been successful for you. If you are hiring a marketing firm to manage your leads, they should really know what they are doing and you shouldn't have to teach them, however, you will still want to pay attention to where your money is being spent. If you are hiring a cold caller or transaction coordinator, they may have some experience, but they don't have experience with you and the way you work and what you specifically need or want or expect from them. It takes a lot of time, energy, and money to build a team, a machine, that can turn out five, ten, or fifty deals a month. With a team of five good people you could do ten to fifteen deals a month, however, with a team of twenty okay people, you could do five deals a month. Find the right people and that is how you will build your team. Be slow to hire and quick to fire. My team has varied from two people all the way up to twelve people and, as I write this book, we are now just a team of six again. Six key players who are dedicated and know what they are doing and how to do it with little supervision can be more successful than a giant team. It will take time, energy, failures, and successes to find the people you want to be part of your team.

Some of the standard roles in a wholesaling team are:

Acquisitions Manager. This is typically the person closing the deals on the front end. They are getting the contract signed with the seller. They are typically paid heavy on commission and low on salary. They will manage other members of the team.

Dispositions Manager. This person is dealing with the end buyer. They are sending out the deal and negotiating with your buyer base. They should have a good understanding of what the end buyers are going to be doing to or with the property. They are typically paid heavy on commission and low on salary.

Transaction Coordinator. This is the hub of information. This is the person who makes sure paperwork is happening, money is moving, and deals are closing when they are supposed to be. This person is typically paid heavy on salary and receives bonuses on closing volume. The more closings you are doing, the more work they will have to do. Organization is key for this role.

Office Manager. Someone has to keep everyone working together, running meetings, and making sure the company goals are being achieved. This person is typically paid heavy on salary and receives bonuses on closing volume.

Leads/Marketing Manager. If you are running a big operation, or even a small one, you have to make sure leads are coming in. This person will typically be tracking your KPIs and will really become the lifeblood of the company. If this person is failing, there won't be leads. This person is typically paid heavy on salary and receives bonuses on closing volume.

Cold callers / Bird dogs / Door knockers / and so on. These roles will see a lot more turnover and definitely will be the less-skilled positions, however, if someone shines, give them more duties and more money. Sing their successes. These roles are hourly and have incentives for closings that they are part of.

Make sure you have the same vision, and when you find that right person bring them on, encourage them, pay them, and grow with them. Your business will always evolve and you will lose team members, you will fire people, people will move, people will quit, people will go off on their own, it is just the nature of this business. As you grow, be prepared for it. Be slow to hire, and quick to fire, it doesn't matter if it is an in-office position or a contract worker doing cold calls. Protect your business.

Your peripheral team can be just as important as your in-house team. By this I mean your title officers, attorneys, Realtors, home inspectors, mortgage professional, tax consultants, credit repair specialist, contractors, etc. You'll find as your business grows, you will need someone you can trust in all of these positions and more. In fact, in some cases you can even get referral fees from these partners of yours, although your first goal should always be to help your client, your seller, with what they truly need. Perhaps one of your sellers is in pre-foreclosure, you get their property under contract and then can refer them to a credit repair specialist? If the seller signs up for their credit repair program, not only have you helped the seller, but the credit repair specialist may pay you a referral fee. Don't expect this from all of these trades as some of them are regulated on what they can do. Additionally, make sure you are partnering up with professionals that are truly looking out for the sellers you recommend to them. Honesty and integrity of your referrals reflects on you, don't tarnish your name and reputation for a quick dollar.

CASH MORE CHECKS

- Be slow to hire and quick to fire.

- Build the team you want, you don't have to do what others do.

- Reward those who do well.

- Hire what you hate or you don't know.

- Focus on your highest income-producing activities, hire out the rest.

- Every team is different.

- Make sure everyone is running the same race with the same goals.

- Every team needs a leader. You are that leader.

- Partner with professionals. Your referrals reflect on you.

CHAPTER 13

Tracking Your Numbers, Did Someone Say KPI?

Key Performance Indicators (KPI) are how you know if you are doing good or bad, if you are reaching your goals and targets, and where you stack up against others in your industry. These can be broad indicators of your company such as "Number of deals closed in the year," all the way to the minutia of such items as "Cost per lead from PPC campaign four." And I can tell you from experience, the more you track your numbers, your results, your expenses, and your return, the better and more efficient you will be with both your time and money. You will have a much clearer picture as to where you are and where you are headed.

It's not just tracking the numbers that is important, but reacting to them as well. My team has weekly Monday meetings and, for our wholesaling department, here are the numbers that are actually reported within the weekly meeting:

- Number of leads received last week

- Number of appointments walked last week

- Number of offers made last week

- Number of properties under contract last week

- Number of wholesale contracts sold last week

If I see that we had twenty-two leads come in last week, but we only walked four appointments, I'm going to question this. If you (or your virtual/JV partners) aren't getting into houses, you are less likely to get contracts. If I see we walked twelve appointments but we had zero contracts signed, I'm going to have to question my sales team as to why they aren't closing deals. Why does this matter? Well, when you start paying for leads, this really matters, because each one of those leads, appointments, and contracts has a cost associated with it and it all starts with your lead generation. These are the minutia that we also track, but just don't report those in the overall meeting. I have separate meetings with my lead acquisition manager and she reports these to me. For example, if we have a marketing campaign that costs $1,000 and it brings in ten leads, each of those leads cost $100. If out of those ten leads we get five appointments, that means each appointment cost $200. And if from those five appointments we get two contracts (that's a closing ratio of twenty percent; five appointments divided by two contracts, another stat we track), each of those contracts cost $500. All those costs started from the original $1,000 cost of that specific marketing campaign. Remember, if you are spending money, you want to make sure it's worth it, and we do this for every one of our campaigns. If I decide I want to spend another $5,000 in marketing, I don't want to just guess where I should put it, I want to put it where I am going to get my biggest and/or most consistent return. Some campaigns you will see more contracts and leads from, but they will be less profitable deals. Other campaigns you will see fewer deals, but more profit. This is why it is important to know your numbers, to know your key performance indicators.

Here are some of the items we track:

- Cost per lead per campaign

- Cost per contract per campaign

- Number of leads per campaign (daily)

- Number of contracts per campaign (weekly)

- Closing ratio of acquisition manager

- Return mail per list

- Monthly, quarterly, and yearly expenses for everything

- Gross profit per deal

- Net profit per deal

- Gross profit per acquisition manager

- Net profit per acquisition manager

There are many items you will want to track, and this list will grow. The most important thing is to actually know how you and your company compare to industry norms. If your acquisitions manager has a closing ratio of twenty percent and others in the industry in your market area have ratios of sixty percent, you may need a better acquisitions manager. If your mailing campaign is leading to a two hundred percent return on cost (it cost $5,000 and you net $10,000) and you find out others mailing to similar lists are getting a six hundred percent return on cost, you may not be closing enough or you may not be getting your contracts at a steep-enough discount to make higher assignment fees or you may not have the best marketing material to drive returns. There are a lot of factors that play into this business and, as you dig into it, you definitely want to network and find friends you can talk to and compare numbers with. This will help both of you. Remember, we have an abundance mentality and there are enough deals out there for everyone. If you expect something that is not possible, you will never be happy and never reach it. Start with your basic reporting and track everything. As you spend money, make sure to view it as individual items you are spending for and make sure it is a wise investment. Build your team on success, reward success, and move on from failure. This is all done by tracking and reporting your KPIs.

CASH MORE CHECKS

- Track your numbers.

- The numbers tell you how your business is doing.

- If something is working, double down on it.

- Hold yourself (and your team) accountable.

- Find out if your targets are reasonable, by making some industry friends.

- If you are spending money, you had better be making money.

CHAPTER 14

Whose Business Is This?

This is your business! It will grow and prosper or shrivel and die depending on how much time, energy, and effort you put into it. It won't be easy, far from it. It will take time to get your first contract signed. Go into any Facebook wholesaling group and just ask the question "How long did it take you to get your first contract?" You'll get answers ranging from a couple of weeks to a couple of years. Everyone's journey is different. Everyone has put different dedication, time, money, and resources into their businesses, so what happened for one person most likely won't happen the same for you. Why? Because this is your business, not theirs!

If you are just starting out in this business, most likely you already have another job and that takes up most of your time. Most likely, you are getting into this business because of the money (that is okay by the way), but most likely you don't have a ton of money to put into marketing right now. Everyone has a different starting point. Some people are comfortable offering someone $40,000 for a house they know is worth $150,000, other people would rather offer $110,000 because they think it is fairer. This is your business. Does the $40,000 offer solve the seller's problem? If yes and you get the deal, then great. You have to treat this as a business. Even though emotions have to be dealt with in this business, you have to look at the numbers and have to do what works for you. Why? Because no one else is going to do it for you.

- If you aren't working, your business isn't working.

- If you aren't answering your phone or picking it up to make calls, your business isn't working.

- If you aren't posting on social media or running ad campaigns, your business isn't working.

- If you aren't knocking on doors and making offers, your business isn't working.

- If you aren't networking with other wholesalers and buyers, your business isn't working.

- If you aren't learning and growing, your business isn't working.

This is your business, it doesn't belong to anyone else. No one is going to do it for you, no one is going to be more in control of your success than you. You have to do this, you have to make this work, you are the one that has to do this business.

This. Is. Your. Business.

Treat people with respect no matter how they treat you. Get rid of the negative and the naysayers because I know if you take action you can do this business. Surround yourself with people that can see you being successful. You do not have the time for naysayers, for unbelievers, for negativity. You will change, your situation will change, your friends will change, you will grow and reach your goals but only if you take action.

Now put this book down, get out there, and start taking action. As you move forward, you may come across different questions and issues. I am here to help and so are other wholesalers and investors across the country. Make sure you join *"The Flipping Blueprint Group"* on Facebook to ask your questions, to get more tips and tricks and to connect with other like-minded individuals. Who knows, you may find your first JV deal there! And if you found value in my words, please share it with others and leave a review wherever you bought the book. If you don't ask for things, you won't get them. Just like I am asking for a review, make sure to ask your sellers and buyers for reviews, too. Now get out there and close some deals.

I am excited to see your success.

If you haven't read *The Flipping Blueprint: The Complete Plan for Flipping Houses and Creating Your Real Estate Investing Business*, find it at all major bookstores and online booksellers.

Don't take my word on it, here's what other readers are saying...

> "I'm not a book reader at all. In fact, I can't remember the last time I read a book in its entirety. This book kept me constantly interested by the excellent content and step-by-step process to becoming a successful real estate investor. Author and active flipper Luke Weber explains his process for flipping houses that will not only give you the tools to become a successful investor but will also keep you from making costly mistakes in the process. I highly recommend reading this book even if you're an experienced flipper yourself."—Kyle F.

> "This book is super informative, easy to read, and lays out the perfect blueprint to start a real estate empire by flipping homes. Luke Weber also opens his vast array of knowledge to his readers via access to him on social media websites. You could not ask more from a writer."—Kenneth J.

> "This book will teach you what you need to know to do fix and flips and I highly recommend it!"—Jason K.

> "Couldn't have picked a better book to read as a beginning investor. The time and money I've saved in the lessons taught in this book have been invaluable. It truly has helped me establish my Blueprint to become

a successful investor. Easy to read and the concepts are broken down in the simplest format. This is a book I will always have at my fingertips and will continue to re-read. Whether you're a beginning investor or seasoned pro, I highly recommend reading this book."— T.J. F.

"Luke's book touches on so many things that are not taught at seminars. Those people charge $25,000+ and there is more information in this one book than multiple seminars combined! I thoroughly enjoyed this book and I can't wait to follow in Luke's footsteps in perfecting my business model. Thank you, Luke, for bringing this to the marketplace. It is truly needed."—Greg S.

"This book is the perfect mix of 'here's how it's done' and 'alright, stop and do it.' I've read many real estate books and this was the first one that actually got me to take action while reading it. And the items that you need to do aren't items like 'wake up tomorrow and have millionaire friends' or 'pull $100k out of your—' (although that's the byproduct of flipping houses. lol). This book isn't overly technical, and you'll grasp the big picture ... By the end, you'll have started building momentum to get going. Recommended."—Kyle K.

"Luke did a great job explaining everything about the process of flipping a house. Definitely is a must read for real estate investors."—Jose O.

"I'm totally new to real-estate investing, and this book has been an invaluable blueprint for me. I read it front to back, and then I went through it again and just followed the instructions at each step. I even followed instructions when it didn't feel right, because I'm gonna trust the expert. And it has been profiting me ever since! Thank you Luke!"—Tim D.

"Easy, fun read filled with great info for the seasoned pro or beginner. Luke talks the talk and walks the walk every day. If you have even a slight interest in flipping, this is a must read."—Steve Q.

"Common sense book, loaded with very good information. Don't spend thousands of dollars to learn real estate like I did. Luke Weber has built an awesome business and wishes to share with anyone. I promote this book. A+"—Steve W.

"Great book! I've heard it takes 10,000 hours to become an expert in anything. I prefer to find the person who has put in the time and follow what they've already done successfully. The book title itself is truth in labeling. This is indeed THE Flipping Blueprint!"—J. D. H.

"This book is perfect for the newbie who wants to get started in flipping houses to the seasoned pro who has done countless deals. Luke lays the book out in an easy-to-follow format from before the deal starts to after it closes. There are countless tips and, above all else, actionable steps that get you on your way. I would definitely recommend this book for anyone involved in real estate. Thank you Mr. Weber for your help along my flipping journey!"—Jay S.

"We are semi-new to investing and were thrilled to read this book! Of all of the education we received from the gurus, this book is more valuable to me than the materials I previously received. Mr. Weber's writing style makes it seem like you are having a conversation with him. He breaks the concepts down for everyone to understand. And by understanding the concepts, the fear lessens. I look forward to his next book!"— Angela G.

"After years of doing research and watching HGTV, this book was a very detailed, to-the-point, simple, hands-on book about house flipping from A—Z. This book gives you the meat and potatoes about how to be a successful real estate investor. I have been recommending this book, and will continue to recommend going forward. Love it!!!!!!!!!"—Darrel S.

"Well presented, pertinent, detailed, and realistic. More than just the typical flip 'motivational' book that gives only a broad outline, this book goes into great detail on the whole process."—Jason M. P.

"I learned a lot about real estate from this book. The author wrote the book in a way to make the information very easy to understand. I am more confident now to enter this industry."—Marvin D.

"I've read probably 20+ books on flipping. This has been my favorite. A lot of other flipping books leave out details or are vague when it comes to discussing financial formulas. Luke writes in an easy-to-follow style that allows the reader to take valuable information away."—David B.

Find *The Flipping Blueprint* wherever books are sold!